DOUGLAS LINDSAY was born in Scotland in 1964 at 2:38am.
It rained.

Some decades later he left to live in Belgium. Meeting his
future wife, Kathryn, he took the opportunity to drop out of reality
and join her on a Foreign & Commonwealth Office posting to
Senegal. It was here that he developed the character of Barney
Thomson, while sitting in an air-conditioned apartment drinking
gin & tonic at eight o'clock in the morning. Since the late 1990s,
he has penned seven books in the Barney series, and several other
crime novels written in a non-traditional style. His first book,
The Long Midnight of Barney Thomson, has been translated into
several languages and will soon be released as the major motion
picture event, *The Legend of Barney Thomson* starring Robert Carlyle,
Emma Thompson and Ray Winstone.

Raised in Cambuslang, scunnered in perpetuity, Lindsay
moved to Estonia the day after the Referendum.

DR IAN SHACKLETON is rumoured to be a figment of his
imagination. Any resemblance to persons living or dead is
unlikely.

By Douglas Lindsay

The Barney Thomson novels
The Long Midnight Of Barney Thomson
The Barber Surgeon's Hairshirt
Murderers Anonymous
The Resurrection Of Barney Thomson
The Last Fish Supper
The Haunting Of Barney Thomson
The Final Cut
The Barbershop Seven (*The Barney Thomson Novel Omnibus*)

Barney Thomson Novellas/Short Stories
The Face Of Death
The Wormwood Code
The End Of Days
Barney Thomson, Zombie Killer
The Curse Of Barney Thomson

The Thomas Hutton Novels
The Unburied Dead
A Plague of Crows
The Blood That Stains Your Hands

Other Novels
Lost in Juarez
Being For The Benefit Of Mr Kite!
A Room With No Natural Light (2015)
We Are The Hanged Man

Short stories
The Case Of The Stained Glass Widow
Santa's Christmas Eve Blues

Non-fiction
For The Most Part Uncontaminated
There Are Always Side Effects
Kids, And Why You Shouldn't Eat More Than One For Breakfast

From #Indyref to Eternity

The battle for a nation, and how proud Scotia
came within a whisker of breaking free

DOUGLAS LINDSAY

with illustrations by
BOB DEWAR

Luath Press Limited
EDINBURGH
www.luath.co.uk

First published 2014

A rapid-response version of this text – a first draft of history
in the making – appeared weekly in *HeraldScotland Online*
between March and September 2014.

ISBN: 978-1-910021-83-5

The paper used in this book is recyclable. It is made from
low chlorine pulps produced in a low energy, low emissions manner
from renewable forests.

Printed and bound by
CPI Antony Rowe, Chippenham

Typeset in Quadraat and MetaPlus
by 3btype.com

Introduction

The Scottish Referendum on independence of 2014 will go down in history as one of the great referendums of 2014.

Of all the words written during the debate, and analysts believe that there were more than 300 million such words, none were more influential than those written in the Shackleton Report, which appeared every Monday morning, for the six months prior to the vote, in the online edition of *The Herald*.

Now the reports, including as they do the numerous insightful, at-the-time, off-the-cuff verbatim quotes from Dr Ian Shackleton of the Glasgow School of Politics and Football, have been collected together into one edition, providing a valuable starting point for historians of the future.

Professor Malcolm Connery
The Glasgow Institute of Special Things
November 2014

31 March 2014

Westminster Vows 'Not to Invade Scotland' In Event of Yes Vote

Despite a reported rise in troop deployments to the north of England, and claims that the British army have begun to send all Scottish soldiers to Afghanistan while deploying English and Welsh troops to Scottish barracks, ministers in Westminster today denied that the UK was getting ready to crush Scotland militarily in the event of a Yes vote in September's Referendum.

A report in the *Guardian* this weekend had quoted one unidentified UK government minister as saying that 'of course England would invade' in the event of a Yes vote. 'Sure, we want to sound reasonable, we don't want to sound like we hate the Scots,' said the unnamed minister. 'However, the reality, as everybody knows, is that we're Tories. We eat babies. We slaughter wild animals out of badness. We want to tax kittens. We make people with no limbs go to juggling academy or lose their benefit. Of course we'll invade.'

Although Scottish Deputy First Minister, Nicola Sturgeon, claimed the No campaign was 'deeply damaged' by the leak, George Osborne and Danny Alexander made a joint appearance, standing on top of a tank as it rolled up the M6, to deny the *Guardian's* story. Asked repeatedly if they were guilty of bluff and bluster, Osborne cracked, 'No, I'm Bluster, he's Bluff,' to hoots of laughter from the assembled press corps.

Speaking to me this morning from his office on the 98th floor of Glasgow's Salmond State Building, Dr Shackleton told me he believed the real losers are the electorate. 'We all know the only honest politician is a dead one,' said Shackleton. 'They're all jockeying for position at the moment. Will England invade? Will they deny Scotland the Pound? Is Alex Salmond's reported Plan B really the reintroduction of the groat? At the moment they're trying to win votes, and as a result truth lies bloody and slaughtered at the feet of the gorilla of political expediency.'

Some political analysts, such as Professor Malcolm Connery, of the Glasgow Institute of Special Things, believe war is inevitable. 'There's just too much unfinished business,' said Connery. 'We haven't forgiven the Clearances, and they haven't forgotten Jim Baxter playing keepie uppie when we handed them their arse at Wembley in '67.'

Later, showing the kind of political insight that only years at Westminster can bring, Scottish Secretary Alistair Carmichael admitted that while some people might vote No, others might vote Yes.

Other Referendum News From The Past Week

Friday 28 March

'It was like Nelson Mandela's release from prison multiplied by VE Day,' says Dr Shackleton, referring to Nick Clegg's triumphant keynote pro-Unionist speech at the Scottish Lib Dem's spring conference.

In the most extraordinary political oration of this, or any other, generation, Mr Clegg told an audience of almost 100,000, packed into the Aberdeen & District Liberal and Working Men's Alliance Social Club, that staying in the UK would be 'the most thrilling thing that happens to any of us in our lifetime.'

'What we're seeing here,' says Dr Shackleton, 'is a further demonstration of the sheer power that lies behind the No campaign. These guys are Big Dogs, and big dogs have big balls. Alex Salmond may have the girth of ten men, but next to the likes of behemoths such as Clegg, he looks like Hen Broon on the Atkins (diet).'

Mr Clegg, fresh from crushing Nigel Farage earlier this week, was in fine form, as he stood on the podium Putinesque, bare-chested and clutching a claymore. There was one awkward slip of the tongue from the Lib Dem leader when he inadvertently referred to he and Danny Alexander 'hammering out the badger.' He quickly apologised, stating that what he in fact meant was that they'd been badgering the hamster together.

Wednesday 26 March 2014

There was another blow for the SNP today as new research revealed that all 790 islands off the coast of Scotland will seek independence for themselves in the event of a Yes vote in September's Referendum. It was already known that the likes of Shetland, Orkney and Millport were exploring their options, but now it seems that independence fever is sweeping the islands, from Berneray and Easdale, to Ailsa Craig, St Kilda and the Bass Rock.

It's not yet known whether the islands will join together as a single nation, to be known as the Federated Islands of The Former United Caledonian Kingdom of (FITF***) Scotland, or whether they will look to be independent from each other. It is the latter case that is already causing headaches throughout Europe.

'Holy merde!' gasped Michel Platini, President of UEFA, 'for sure if this happens, we'll need to start the qualifying rounds for Euro 2024 last year.'

'It was inevitable,' says Dr Shackleton. 'We're in the viral age. Ideas catch on and sweep around the world in minutes. From Miley Cyrus photobombing David Cameron at Wimbledon, to Alex Salmond swinging butt naked on a wrecking ball, images and ideas instantly become that day's zeitgeist. Today it's the notion of independent islands. The SNP have opened Pandora's box, and now global fragmentation leading to annihilation of life on earth is inevitable.'

Monday 24 March 2014

With two years to go until the date that the SNP hope to be able to declare Scotland an independent nation, deputy leader of the party, Nicola Sturgeon, today announced that a new Scottish Constitution would be unveiled before Holyrood goes into summer recess.

Entitled Declaration of Arbroath II and written on parchment made from the wooden legs of Highlanders enslaved after the Battle of Culloden, the new constitution will, said Sturgeon, 'light a fire under Westminster's arse, and show them we mean business.'

New laws enshrined in the constitution will allow citizens the right to graze sheep on any golf course owned by Donald Trump and see Archie Gemmill's goal against Holland declared a UNESCO World Heritage Site.

With weekend polls showing the Yes vote catching the No vote, and with the Yes campaign making an Ally McLeod-esque assumption that once someone has decided to vote Yes they won't change their mind, the mood in their camp is ebullient.

'We will close the wall up with the English dead,' said one SNP insider, 'and tonight we feast on two-for-one lamb steaks from Scotmid.'

The latest poll in today's Scotsman shows voters split nearly fifty-fifty between those who think politicians should be seen less often on television, and those who think they are already seen too much.

7 April 2014

Independent Scotland Set To Lose The Right To Call Itself Scotland

With news that the opinion polls are closing, amid SNP hopes that they could be leading most national surveys by mid-summer, David Cameron today stepped up plans to make sure that an independent Scotland would not have the right to use its name should it ever get to have its own seat at the United Nations.

Top political analyst, Dr Ian Shackleton, believes that Westminster is considering several possibilities to legally lay claim to the name 'Scotland' prior to independence, allowing them to deny Holyrood its use in the event of a Yes vote, much in the way that the Greeks have maintained with Macedonia.

Options being considered include:

- designating the area around Berwick in the north of England as the Unitary Council Authority of Scotland
- re-naming the Falkland Islands, Scotland
- producing a cheese in the north of England named

Scotland, and registering its legitimacy with the European Union

- buying a certificate claiming ownership of the name Scotland on the Internet for £1

Continued suggestions, however, that Scotland will need to become known as The Former Yugoslav Republic of Scotland – FYR Scotland – seem unlikely. Westminster, it is rumoured, will be pushing for the new nation to be known as The Former United Caledonian Kingdom of Scotland – or F*** Scotland, as it will be known if it ever gets to take its place in New York.

'There is no doubt,' Dr Shackleton told me this morning, speaking from his 98th floor office in the glittering Burj Salmond, overlooking Glasgow's celebrated financial district, 'that the F*** Scotland campaign is gaining ground in Westminster. Just remember that it was the Tories who started the Opium Wars, massacred Zulus, re-introduced child labour in the '80s and were the primary cause for Scotland losing 1–0 to Costa Rica at Italia '90. They will stop at nothing.'

Friends of political insiders say that the campaign against Scotland is only just beginning, and that in the next few weeks the government in Westminster intends to tell Scotland that in the event of a Yes vote:

- it can't use the colour blue for its national sports teams
- Flower of Scotland will need to include verses about Culloden, the Darien Scheme and Wembley '61
- Buckfast Abbey will not be granted a licence to export fortified wine
- the whole of F*** Scotland will be carpet-bombed by American troops 'looking for something to do' after withdrawing from Afghanistan
- Scotland could be bricked off and declared a penal colony

In response, Holyrood insiders have repeated claims that First Minister Salmond is aiming to push for Derby in a new spring offensive.

Other Referendum News From The Past Week

Sunday 6 April

Under-fire UK government Culture Secretary, Maria Miller, can have a job 'any time she feels like it' in the Scottish government, Alex Salmond said today. Referencing the popularity of Miller north of the border, as well as that of many of her Westminster colleagues, Salmond said a future independent Scotland would look to build a Gordon Brown-esque Government Of All the Talents (GOAT) administration.

'Government by GOAT worked brilliantly for Brown,' said Salmond, as he spoke this weekend from New York, where he is launching Braveheart Week across the US. 'That's what we need to do in Edinburgh. Suck in people with talent from all over, and govern as a kind of cross-party autonomous collective. If Maria is somehow forced out by a desperate opposition and a baying press corps, she's welcome at Holyrood. We'll find her a seat, nae bother.'

Salmond is also rumoured to be eyeing up other top Tories, popular north of the border, but who sometimes come in for a rough time in Englandshire.

Dr Shackleton is unsurprised by this new approach. 'Look at guys like Eric Pickles and Jeremy Hunt,' he said to me. 'People in Scotland love them, and yet the English don't appreciate what they've got. And Michael Gove – sure, he sounds posh, but of course he's as Scottish as early World Cup exits and a male life expectancy of 57.'

Maria Miller was unavailable for comment, but a statement released by her people indicated that while she had heard of Scotland, she wasn't entirely sure she could place it on the map.

Tuesday 1 April

While levels of acrimony and bitterness between the Yes and No campaigns in the Scottish Referendum have grown exponentially, there's one thing on which they all agree. Politicians, pundits, political analysts, commentators, party insiders and crazy people on the

Internet have never had so much fun. As a result, regardless of the outcome of the vote on 18 September, it seems certain that Scotland will have another Referendum next year.

The likes of Johann Lamont, John Swinney and Nicola Sturgeon have become Scotland's answer to Beyonce and J-Zed, with constant demands on their time, be it for modelling contracts, celebrity TV chat shows, or appearing naked in rock videos with Katy Perry.

'You can understand how these politicians have become attached to the celebrity lifestyle,' says Dr Shackleton. 'One minute they're grubbing along in the dirt with a name recognition equivalent to some guy who was in an episode of *CSI Bishopbriggs* once, and the next they're wife-swapping at drunken Hollywood parties. Consider Ruth Davidson. She received about 12 votes at the last election, yet now she's considered a political heavyweight of the calibre of Aung San Suu Kyi, and she's been linked romantically with Angelina Jolie.'

While it's not yet clear what question will be asked at next year's Referendum, insiders believe that if the winning margin in the independence vote is less than 1%, the vote will be repeated in an effort to get a more clearcut result. 'That's what everyone's after,' says Shackleton. 'We all want exactly the same thing next year. The public especially, they can't get enough of it.'

However, if September's vote sees one side getting their arse handed to them, then all kinds of questions could be on the table, including:

- should Scotland's national anthem be Flower of Scotland, Highland Cathedral or the Bay City Rollers' Shang-a-lang?
- Should Scotland apply to join Warsaw Pact II?
- Should curling replace football as the national sport?
- Should Scotland just stop playing rugby because, to be honest, it's getting embarrassing?

Speaking from the set of Tom Cruise's *Top Gun II*, where he's appearing as Maverick's new sidekick, Donut, Alex Salmond was excited at the thought of repeating the whole Referendum experience. 'I'm going balls out for this. It's awesome. Look, I need to dash, I'm doing *Celebrity Man Versus Food* in ten minutes.'

'One thing's for sure,' said Shackleton. 'When this thing's over, it'll be like the whole nation has died. The morning of 19 September is going to be the flattest day in history, even for the winners. Nobody's going to know what to do with themselves.'

7 April 2014

Cameron Finally Agrees
To Meet Salmond Head On

After months of goading from the Scottish First Minister and the Yes campaign, UK Prime Minister, David Cameron, has finally agreed to meet Alex Salmond head to head. Insiders believe that Mr Cameron had approved the meeting in principle last year, but that there has been several months of behind-the-scenes haggling over what format the live TV clash should take.

While Mr Salmond's team has been pushing for a two-man debate on the BBC hosted by Radio 4 sex symbol, Jim Naughtie, Mr Cameron's advisors have been reluctant to let him anywhere near that kind of situation.

'It's understandable,' said Dr Shackleton, speaking to me this morning from his office on the 98th floor of the spectacular Salmond Barbican in the heart of Glasgow's Presbyterian Quarter 'Why would Cameron go on TV in Scotland? Virtually everyone north of the border believes he was cloned in the early '80s from a malignant cell plucked from the burned remains of Thatcher's heart. Every time he opens his mouth, a No voter's soul turns to dust.'

After rejecting various other formats, including a Question Time Special with the leaders of all the main parties, and a hustings type debate with Salmond and Cameron taking questions from the floor, the two sides have finally settled on a best-of-5 Mario Kart challenge. Friends of political insiders understand that the breakthrough came some weeks ago, and that the delay since then has been down to wrangling over who gets to be Donkey Kong.

'Whatever anyone says, this is bang on,' added Dr Shackleton. 'If western society was a computer game, it'd be Mario Kart. It captures the zeitgeist of these hedonistic, frivolous, crapulent, wasteful times to perfection.'

As the Referendum debate moves towards its extraordinary climax and voters are whipped into a frenzy of excitement, TV executives are known to be considering many more banner prime time events, including:

- Johann Lamont & Gordon Brown v Nicola Sturgeon & Alex Salmond mixed naked mud wrestling contest over 15 rounds.

- *Come Dine With Me* Referendum Special, with Alistair Darling, Ruth Davidson, Lord Robertson and Frankie Boyle

- Scotland Rugby XV v rUK VIIs

- A *Who Do You Think You Are?* special with David Cameron, wherein he discovers his great great great great great grandfather set out for Scotland once, but turned back at Watford

- *I'm A Celebrity, Get Me Out Of Here!* with the likes of Malcolm Rifkind, Eddi Reader, Kenny MacAskill and Eddie Izzard marooned on a remote Scottish island and made to eat deep fried sheep's testicles

'One thing's for sure,' said Shackleton. 'We'll be seeing a lot more of all these politicians over the next few months. The public can't get enough of them. Isn't it great?'

Other Referendum News From The Past Week

Sunday 13 April

Speaking to the SNP spring conference yesterday in Aberdeen, Alex Salmond blasted the No campaign as being the 'most miserable, negative, depressing and thoroughly boring campaign in modern political history, modelled on Craig Levein's tactics against the Czech Republic in Prague.'

Arguing that the No campaign better up their game or else Scotland is going to become independent and 'I'm going to brick myself,' Mr Salmond said that listening to an endless stream of Piccadilly Scots badmouth the old country was driving countless undecided voters into the Yes camp.

'The No Campaign is like watching Craig Levein multiplied by Craig Brown,' continued Salmond. 'You try to make sure you don't lose, and then you lose. At least with us you'll get a bit of the Ally McLeod. Before you lose.'

Dr Shackleton believes it a bold move from the SNP leader. 'It's ballsy, there's no question. It's one thing to slag off your opponent, that's what politicians do. But to give them a report card, pointing out what they're doing wrong, so that they can change their game plan and bring people off the bench... Curious. Salmond must be really worried he's going to win.'

In other news from the SNP conference, Deputy Leader of the SNP, Nicola Sturgeon, defended the demolition of Ibrox Stadium as part of the Commonwealth Games opening ceremony. 'It's had a good run,' she told conference-goers, 'but it's about time it was put out its misery.'

Thursday 10 April

Lord Robertson's 5 Worst Things That Will Happen As A Result Of A YES Vote

5 There will be a worldwide blight on wheat crops, meaning no flour, there will be no batter for deep frying, and therefore NO FISH SUPPERS.

4 Russia will annex Caithness, NATO will send in troops under the command of Baron Münchhausen of Port Ellen, and Scotland will become the bloody battlefield that is the prelude to World War III.

3 Scotland will become Syria multiplied by Bosnia, there will be ethnic and tribal division, the country will splinter into a hundred fiefdoms, and rivers will run red with blood.

2 Baroness Thatcher will rise from the dead and feast on the charred flesh of barbecued children.

1 There will be ethnic cleansing of gingers.

Tuesday 1 April

UK Chancellor, Gideon Osborne, sought to draw a line under the row over Treasury recommendations that an independent Scotland should not be allowed to use the Pound by admitting on *Newsnight* that 'of course a currency union would be fine, but who cares, man? They want out? Fine, on you go suckers, leave, but don't expect to be able to come home and use the bathroom, that's all I'm saying.'

Confirming SNP claims that the No campaign were bigging up the potential economic pitfalls of Scottish independence, Mr Osborne continued, 'Yes, we make shit up. OMG! The Pope's a Catholic, bears shit in the woods, and politicians will say anything in the name of political expediency. Big deal. Well, I'm telling you the truth now: we lied.'

Commentators, analysts and crazy people on the Internet were surprised by this outburst of honesty, but Dr Shackleton believes it heralds a new openness in the debate over Scottish independence, and throughout British politics in general.

In other political developments, as truth-telling broke out across the entire political spectrum:

- Alex Salmond revealed that he already had a currency Plan B, but was saving his Scottish Imperial Shekel proposal until after the vote
- Boris Johnson admitted he's never even heard of Scotland. He also acknowledged that he's desperate to be Prime Minister and is intent on launching internecine strife within the Conservative Party, that will see Osborne, Gove and Cameron dead, their heads on spikes outside Party HQ as a warning to others
- David Miliband says he's actively trying to have his brother assassinated
- Alistair Darling admitted that he never wanted to be a politician anyway, and that he's always wanted to be a lumberjack

21 April 2014

Who Will Be Scotland's First Prime Minister?

Some analysts say that voters in Scotland shouldn't even be considering the identity of their first Prime Minister until after a Yes vote has been secured. However, with the polls closing on a weekly basis, and with Rangers more or less the only Scottish business left as a member of the CBI as the latest fiasco engulfs the floundering No campaign, some political insiders, such as Dr Ian Shackleton, believe that this is precisely the kind of issue that Scots must address in advance.

'Of course, this is a legacy vote,' said Dr Shackleton as he spoke to me this morning in his office on the 98th floor of the magnificent Salmond 101 in Glasgow's flourishing east end. 'It's about the next thousand years not the next five minutes. Nevertheless, voters need to think about this issue. It's unavoidable.'

Dr Shackleton talked me through the runners and riders.

SNP

Alex Salmond: 1/5

'It's his to lose,' says Shackleton. 'As clear a favourite to be Scotland's first PM as Mandela was to be the first President of post-Apartheid South Africa. But we Scots have a way of hitting the corner flag from five yards out in front of an open goal. The favourites tag rarely sits well with us. Mr Salmond should watch where he puts his feet. Although to be fair, he can't actually see his feet.'

Nicola Sturgeon: 200/1

Salmond's able Sancho Panza, Sturgeon is in prime position to take his place when he chooses to step down. Odds fell away dramatically, however, after the 'handbags at yawn' debate debacle with Johann Lamont. 'No doubt that Sturgeon was the big loser there,' says Shackleton. 'They both looked bad, but everyone already knew that Lamont was like David Beckham at a convention of Stephen Hawkings. This pitched Sturgeon at the same level.'

LABOUR

'It'll be interesting,' says Shackleton, admittedly stretching the definition of the word, 'to see what the likes of Douglas Alexander and Big Gordon Brown do. Will they look to get an English seat and remain at Westminster, or will they come home and throw their hat into the Holyrood ring?'

Johann Lamont: 140,000,000/1

'Could possibly find her place in a future Labour government buying the biscuits,' says Shackleton.

Big Gordon Brown: 7/1

No one knows what would happen if Big Gordon Brown decided to jump into the tiny swimming pool of Scottish politics. Shackleton, however, believes his presence could be a game changer. 'People love him for his winning smile and witty one-liners. It's possible that enough time might have elapsed since he oversaw the total cataclysmic collapse of the British economy that voters will have forgotten that he was rubbish.'

Wendy Alexander: 20/1

'Wendy Alexander is the shark in *Jaws*. You can't see her, and she seems to have disappeared, but she's still out there, biding her time. The SNP just need to hope they have a Robert Shaw in their midst when she returns. Sure, people can't stand her, but on the other hand you want your Prime Minister to have giant balls.'

CONSERVATIVE

Ruth Davidson: n/a

So unelectable, she is even known to spoil her own ballot paper.

Rory Stewart: 25,000/1

Already has an English seat in Westminster, so doesn't need to come north. 'Nevertheless,' says Shackleton, 'his life has been this kind of strange 19th century Boy's Own adventure, and not everyone hates him yet because they don't know who he is. Could just be the chap to push the number of Conservative voters in Scotland back into double figures.'

LIBDEM

Willie Rennie: Billions/1

'You can see why we are where we are,' says Shackleton. 'On the one hand you have Alex Salmond; on the other, Lamont, Davidson and Rennie. The era of the heavyweight politician in Scotland is over. We're moving into the Blancmange Period.'

Danny Alexander: Billions/1

'The only way Danny Alexander has a future in politics,' says Shackleton, 'is if he gets the Army on his side and mounts a coup. It's an actual statistical fact that no one currently living will ever vote for Danny Alexander again, ever.'

'Let there be no counting of chickens,' says Shackleton. 'There's nowhere like Scotland for taking a foregone conclusion and missing the hole from twelve inches. If we get a Yes vote in September, the lead-up to the country's first ever General Election will be like Kennedy v Nixon multiplied by the X Factor.'

Other Referendum News From The Past Week

Thursday 17 April

In what analysts are calling the #Indyref smoking gun, doubts were cast today over the future of the current Scotland football team, when sources deep within world governing body FIFA indicated that if the country becomes independent, it will be required to reapply for membership.

While most consider that membership to be a foregone conclusion, it does mean that Scotland will be starting again from the bottom of the heap. As a result, if the current team qualifies for Euro 2016 in France, they will then be barred from taking that place, as Scotland will have become independent a few months previously.

'People assume,' said a friend of a FIFA insider, 'that because Scotland already have a team, that they will continue their membership. Nothing could be further from the truth. The current membership of the four individual UK countries is anomalous, and governed by very particular provisions. If Scotland becomes independent, then those provisions no longer apply, and Scotland for sure will need to start once more from the bottom. They are currently ranked 22nd in the world, but the new Scotland will be ranked 207th, alongside Bhutan and the Turks & Caicos Islands.'

'It could be years before we recover,' says Dr Shackleton, 'if indeed we ever do. This could be the final nail in the coffin of Scottish football. In independence terms it might seem trivial, but there's no doubt it's a momentum stopper. For the first time in several months, this morning the Yes campaign are biting into a stale doughnut.'

Former Scotland manager Craig Brown said, 'As long as we put ten men behind the ball, the Turks & Caicos shouldn't give us any problems.'

Tuesday 15 April

As the row over the future of the Trident submarine programme escalated, Russian President, Vladimir Putin, today took time out of his busy schedule destabilising Ukraine to get involved in the discussion over the future of the defence of the UK.

Addressing a crowd of cheering oligarchs in Moscow's Red Square, while standing bare-chested on the head of a live bear, Putin recalled the glory days of the Cold War. 'Those were the good times,' he told the assembled masses. 'The world knew where it stood. Europe was a place of peace, and one of the bedrocks of that solidity was the UK. Now, just as we in Russia are working on plans to implement Cold War II, Scotland threatens to remove that bedrock. Breaking up the UK would be catastrophic.'

Pointing out that there are over three thousand Russian speakers in Scotland, Putin said that if there were signs of destabilisation, 'our troops would be forced to invade Scotland to protect them. We wouldn't want to do it, but we have a duty to safeguard the lives of Russian speakers everywhere.'

Asked if the term 'Russian speaker' applied to some wee fellow called Malky from Paisley who decided to learn Russian at night school for a few weeks to meet women, and whose vocabulary didn't extend much beyond *spasiba*, *nyet* and *Zenit St Petersburg*, Putin admitted that Malky was known to him, and that Russia would do everything in its power to make sure he was safe.

Later, Putin spoke wistfully, as he crushed the head of a Dagestani separatist between his thumb and forefinger while cuddling a puppy. 'Cold War II is going to be great for everyone. The good times are coming back. Scotland, however, should beware. If the life of so much as one person who knows the Russian for *glasnost* is put at risk, we will be forced to launch an invasion.'

28 April 2014

Panicking Better Together Make Pact With Four Horsemen Of The Apocalypse

A strange feeling of Groundhog Day has settled over the campaign, news cycles inevitably melding into one another, the words and faces barely changing.

Business Leader A states that Scotland will be fine post-independence; the Yes campaign nod sagely while the No campaign mutter and grumble. Business Leader B states that independence would be catastrophic; the Yes campaign ridicule, the No campaign praise his perceptiveness. Day after endless day the public endures, as if walking through an arid desert beneath the baking sun of the politician's forced smile, Darling's eyebrows blending inexorably into Sturgeon's nippy sweetie grimace.

'It's all good for the Yes vote,' says Dr Ian Shackleton of the Glasgow School of Politics and Football. Speaking to me this morning from his 98th floor office in the magnificent Empire Biscuit Building in the heart of the city's financial sector, Shackleton sees the tide of the campaign flowing only one way. 'It doesn't matter whether the story is for or against, it all serves to normalise the notion of Scottish independence, which is what this lengthy debate has been about.'

Now, while refusing to admit that they're starting to panic, news has emerged from Better Together that they have made a pact with The Four Horsemen Of The Apocalypse. After months of being accused of negative campaigning, it seems they are determined to finally embrace the label.

'See the Yes campaign,' Johann Lamont will tell a conference of businessmen later today in Brechin, 'they're consistently negative about the Union. That's fine apparently. But see as soon as we're negative about breaking up the Union, we're the bad guys. Well, if they think we're negative, we'll give them negative. It's about time we got biblical on their ass.'

While it's not thought that the Four Horsemen will be available to work on the campaign full time – due to other commitments in Ukraine, South Sudan, the Central African Republic and across the Levant – they will make several speeches warning of the dangers of independence over the coming weeks, and will act in an advisory capacity on negativity up until 18 September.

'Is Britain all that Great?' Lamont will continue. 'Probably not. But it's more A Bit Shit Britain than Utterly Atrocious Britain. The people of Scotland need to be told that there is a vastly increased danger of death, war, pestilence and famine in the event of a Yes vote. Is it negative of me to say this? Maybe it is. Bite me.'

In the face of the No campaign's new approach, the First Minister was in belligerent mood, immediately accusing his opponents of bullying by seeking the support of four apocalyptic harbingers of the last judgment. 'These people don't even have a vote,' he told *Good Morning Scotland*.

Other Referendum News From The Past Week

Saturday 26 April

The man in charge of the CBI in Scotland, although no one is entirely sure who that is, today admitted that the CBI's approach to Scottish independence had so far been made largely by consulting Chinese fortune cookies.

'The fortune cookies have been successful for us over the years,' said the unidentified man. 'Yes, admittedly there was the financial crash of 2008, which we didn't see coming. And we had Rangers pegged to win the Champions League three of the last four years, but those blips aside, we were pretty confident.'

The Yes campaign have watched with undisguised pleasure over the last couple of weeks as CBI Scotland have repeatedly shot the No campaign in the face, one public relations disaster piled on another. However, political analysts, such as Dr Shackleton, believe the Yes campaign would do well do consider the CBI fiasco a cautionary tale, rather than a reason for celebration.

'Just remember,' said Shackleton, 'that the people at the centre of the CBI debacle, just like those running the hapless No campaign, are Scottish. These people will still be here, making a total arse of everything they touch, regardless of the outcome of the vote.'

CBI Scotland have confirmed that they will continue to make shit up as they go along for the foreseeable future.

Friday 25 April

The debate took an ominous twist this morning when a leaked Foreign & Commonwealth Office memo revealed a secret plan to offer Scotland to Russia in the event of a Yes vote. The memo, written by a Whitehall mandarin, but signed off by Foreign Secretary, William Hague, outlines a strategy that would see Scotland handed over to the Russian Federation in the interim period following the vote, while the country remained part of the UK.

The FCO memo reveals that as soon as a Yes vote happens, approaches would be made to Russia, offering up Scotland in return for an end to Russian aggression in the east, against Poland, the Baltic states or even Germany. The UK would then use this as a bargaining chip within the EU, in order to put their membership on a more favourable footing.

'That's what this is all about,' said Shackleton. 'They don't care about Scotland, they never did. Most of them don't even know where it is. They've been looking for a Yes vote all along, which is why the No campaign has been so utterly shit. They're doing it on purpose. Now Putin's playing into the Tories' hands, and Cameron is going to tie it all together and use it as leverage within the EU, crushing UKIP in the process. With the Russian military on England's northern border, they'll have to bolster defences up there, spending huge amounts of money in the north, which will make the Tories a political force right across the country. This is Cameron's way of guaranteeing centuries of non-stop Tory rule in England. It's genius.'

Under the terms of the memo:

- Russia would have naval bases at Rosyth, Faslane, Aberdeen and Kinlochbervie
- The currency question would be cleared up by Scotland using the Rouble
- The Scottish football team would be subsumed into Russia, ending years of Scottish football dominance
- Russian would replace Gaelic as the secondary language of road signs that no one understands

Tuesday 22 April

The debate exploded into life today with another intervention from everyone's favourite elephant in the room, Gordon Brown, as the former Prime Minister brought north the message that an independent Scotland would sink beneath the waves of a pensions crisis, and that every single Scottish man and woman would die poverty-stricken, broken and alone, living in a disused croft in the Campsie Fells, with an outside toilet and no wifi coverage.

The man who sold Britain's gold, and instigated the UK's pension crisis in the first place while plunging the country into trillions of pounds worth of debt, used all his experience of turning an economy into a train wreck to lecture Scotland on just how dreadful things could be without people like him in charge of their finances.

During the seven-hour speech to students at the University of Glasgow, Mr Brown outlined four steps that would see the Scottish economy crumble upon independence, as the nation fell into a burning pit, easy prey for the empire-building vultures of the modern world.

- After only one year the pensions bill will outstrip income from oil, wind farms, tourism and Tennent's by over £275billion (or over 10 trillion Scottish Imperial Shekels, as the currency will be by then)
- burdened with pensions debt, the Scottish government will introduce a ground-breaking forced euthanasia law, killing everyone over the age of 60
- despite ridding themselves of the pensions hindrance, it will be too late for the economy, which will already be like Greece multiplied by Iceland. Squared.
- Scotland will be bought over by China. China, in the ultimate act of consumerist revenge, will start getting 4 year-old Scottish children to

manufacture cheap, plastic crap toys for the Chinese market

Dr Shackleton is in no doubt that Big Gordon's intervention will have a decisive effect on the electorate. 'Voters in general, and in particular those in Scotland, tend to live their lives largely in ignorance of political realities. What they need is for people like Big Gordon to tell them how to think. It always helps.'

5 May 2014

Will Scots Still Be Able To Watch Dr Who, And Other Questions

With just over four months to go until polling day, Dr Ian Shackleton of the Glasgow School of Politics and Football tackles the burning questions of the week, giving you, the voter, all the information you'll need to come to an informed choice.

Q **In the event of a Yes vote, what will happen to Berwick Rangers?**

A No one knows. However, the chances are that FIFA will stick their noses in and the Wee Gers will be forced from Scottish football. There's a rumour they could be parachuted into the English Championship, as that's generally considered the equivalent of Scotland's League Two.

Q **If there is a No vote, is it likely that Westminster would use the victory like Cumberland after Culloden, to crush the Scots, stripping them of their traditions and heritage?**

A Probably. A recently-leaked Westminster memo

revealed that in the event of a No vote, Scots would be made to bow before David Cameron, or die. Many analysts predict that Westminster would sell Scotland to China to help pay off the current £1.7trillion UK national debt. The same analysts believe that if Scotland becomes independent it will quickly sink, and will sell itself to China. Either way, Scotland will soon be part of China.

Q Did Alex Salmond really call Scotland a 'nation of drunks'?

A No one knows. As soon as the story broke and journalists tried to get hold of the tape of the interview, they found a fifteen-second section had been erased. The scandal quickly became known as DidSalmondCallScotlandANationOfDrunksGate, although the moniker failed to catch on.

Q Are these politicians ever going to just stop talking?

A No. Like the old question about a tree falling in a forest not making any noise if there's no one there to hear it, most politicians believe that unless they're on the television embracing the philosophy of verbal diarrhoea every night, no one knows they exist. Sadly, regardless of the outcome of the vote, none of them are shutting up any time soon.

Q In the event of a Yes vote, will Scots still be able to watch Dr Who?

A Of course. Indeed, it's thought that Stephen Moffat will insist on the production of *Dr Who* being moved full time to Glasgow, with Peter Capaldi and David Tennant rotating in the role of the Doctor for the next fifty years. Also, *Sherlock* will move to 221b Sauchiehall Street, with Gerard Butler playing the lead.

Q If Westminster bloody-mindedly stick to their guns and don't allow iScotland use of the Pound, what is the SNP's current Plan B?

A No one knows. However, a recent secret internal SNP memo revealed that they are considering plans to introduce the Independent Scottish Imperial Shekel (ISIS).

Q What will become of Trident in the event of a Yes vote?

A No one knows. The SNP insist on its removal, but despite their denials, it might well become tied up in a deal involving currency, national debt, the BBC and Andy Murray. Or perhaps the SNP will hand the facility over to Russia as part of a deal with the First Minister's new BFF, Vladimir Putin.

Q We've had contrasting assessments from S&P and Moody's. What is iScotland's credit rating likely to be?

A Pick a letter of the alphabet and triple it, and you'll be as close as anyone else. Those people just make that shit up as they go along.

Q **Following his catastrophically inept handling of the Better Together campaign, will Alistair Darling ever work again?**

A Given that he's an entrenched part of the establishment with friends and contacts in the highest levels of politics and business, the chances are that his inadequacies will be swept under the carpet, like so many before him, and he will continue to make millions and die a rich, entitled man, while his countrymen live in squalor and despair. The next time you feel pity for him because he's so embarrassingly inept, don't.

Q **I'm thinking of going to Blackpool on holiday. Will I need a passport?**

A Go to Millport instead. It's closer, and the views of the nuclear power station are unparalleled.

Q **iScotland: Land of milk and honey, or boulevard of broken dreams?**

A Could go either way. In truth, it would likely end up somewhere in between. A bit pish, but not as bad as Somalia. Which is like most places really.

Other Referendum News From The Past Week

Saturday 3 May

The tide turned dramatically in Scotland's Referendum debate this week with the revelation that a new grassroots movement of millionaires in favour of the Union has suddenly appeared. Millionaire businessman, Malcolm McMalcolm, wept openly in a video posted on the movement's new website, BordersAreForLosers.com.

'This is a difficult time for millionaires,' says Sir Malcolm, struggling to hold back the tears, before finally sobbing histrionically. 'There are so many of us whose wealth is based on the Union. It's time for millionaires to stand together and speak as one.'

While no one knows exactly how many millionaires there are in Scotland, Dr Shackleton believes that it's not so much the numbers that matter, but that they have at last chosen to speak.

'Most ordinary people are fed up with the campaign, fed up hearing from politicians and celebrities,' he told me this morning, as we spoke in his office on the 98th floor of the towering Burj Cullen Skink in the heart of the city's Soup District. 'They're even fed up hearing from ordinary people. What they've been waiting for is the input of millionaire businessmen, because that's the voice that really counts.'

On the website there are numerous videos of ordinary millionaires speaking about how much the Union means to them, most of whom spontaneously cry at the suggestion of the UK breaking apart.

'This is a real grassroots movement,' says Sir Malcolm. 'We'd all been having conversations in our private members clubs and on our Lear jets and in Cannes and the like, when suddenly we realised we were all saying the same thing. So I called up my pal Biffy in Verbier, and BordersAreForLosers.com was born.'

'Thank God the millionaires have spoken,' said one ordinary person in a street in Glasgow this morning. 'Now, at last, we know what to do.'

Wednesday 30 April

A leaked memo has revealed that leading Westminster-based, Labour Party Scots, such as Douglas Alexander, Big Gordon Brown and Alistair Darling, will all seek to play a significant political role in an independent Scotland in the event of a Yes vote. The memo, written by a friend of a Labour Party insider, acknowledges that the current party in Scotland 'is a total train wreck, by the way', and that there will be a major push to make Alexander the leader of Scottish Labour in the nation's first election after independence.

'Gradually the smoke begins to clear,' said Dr Shackleton. 'Until now we've been unsure what the Westminster Scots would do in the event of a Yes vote. Would they try to get an English seat and stay or would they come home? Alexander, for example, has been the UK's Foreign Secretary-in-waiting for some years now. Yet, he'll no longer be British, so how can he represent their government?'

The memo makes clear that the Scots will not be welcome in the UK parliament and will return home to tackle the SNP head on. Few political analysts are surprised that Alexander will be chosen to be the new face of Scottish Labour.

'He's young, he's gorgeous, and the rumour is that he's hung like a mammoth. Women love him. By 2016, Alex Salmond will have been First Minister for nine years. The voters will be like, enough already, just stop talking! Wee Douglas, on the other hand, will be a relative stranger.

'Suddenly the SNP have a choice to make. Lose the Referendum vote, thereby continuing the status quo; and with any Labour politician of quality – as well as Margaret Curran – going to Westminster, the SNP will be more or less guaranteed decades in charge of a devolved Holyrood government.

'Or they win the Referendum, and risk immediately losing power when the Labour big guns come home, and the electorate return to their Labour-voting roots. It's a tough call.'

Insiders believe that Salmond has already started a subversive campaign to get people to vote No. Having earlier this week praised Vladimir Putin and threatened the EU with Cod War II, he is expected to:

- make a speech in which he calls President Mugabe of Zimbabwe 'my brother'
- sign a bilateral pact of 'mutual support' with Syria's President Assad
- threaten to invest heavily in submarines and sink all EU fishing vessels anywhere in the world
- offer Boris Johnson the position of Mayor of Edinburgh.

12 May 2014

Better Together Laugh In The Face Of Oil Fund Fiasco

As the storm begins to grow over the UK's lack of an oil fund, making it the only oil-producing country besides Iraq not to have one, the Better Together campaign finally stepped into the row this weekend and took the argument to the opposition.

'People compare us to Iraq like it's a bad thing,' said one Better Together insider. 'Yes, Norway have invested in the future. Yes, they have this £500 billion oil fund. But what if tomorrow they get knocked down by a bus? Nobody's thought about that, have they? They can't take it with them.'

The oil fund smoking gun exploded in the face of the No campaign on Sunday with revelations that former government economist, Professor Gavin McGavin of the Glasgow Institute of Special Things, advised the Labour government of the 1970s that Britain should 'do everything exactly the same as Norway or else they'd turn into a bottom-dwelling, failed state, feeding off the rancid, leftover scrapings of American hegemony.'

As a result, the SNP have published a ten-point plan, outlining their vision for the future of oil revenue management in Scotland, including:

- establish and grow an oil fund
- use the money to retake northern England
- distribute doughnuts to the poor

Crack political analyst, Dr Ian Shackleton, is unsurprised that the oil fund issue has finally burst to the surface. 'Like most things, it's easy to lay the blame squarely at the door of the Thatcher government,' he told me this morning, as he sipped a contemplative moccachino in his sumptuous 98th floor office in Burj Khalifa II in the heart of Glasgow's glittering boom-and-bust sector. 'Professor McGavin may have given his advice to the Labour government, but they had nothing to spare. In the late '70s, Britain couldn't afford to buy the biscuits. The '80s were a different matter, however. We were awash with cash, yet the Tories chose to spend the money on the carpet bombing of mining communities in Fife.'

No campaigners, however, say that it's too simplistic to say that Scotland could just magically turn into Norway overnight. 'For a kick-off,' said one friend of a No campaign insider, 'they speak Norwegian. No one understands anything they're saying. Somebody says something, and you're like... what?'

It's crushing arguments such as this that are keeping the Yes campaign trailing in the polls.

While the Nationalist campaign will push for the oil fund discussion to continue to play a major part in the on-going Referendum debate, Dr Shackleton thinks that ultimately it will have limited effect.

'Yes, perhaps the Thatcher government should have set up an oil fund. But in a way, it's old news. Let's not forget, Mrs Thatcher will always be known as the Prime Minister who walked to work on a carpet of dismembered, screaming children. The fact that she didn't enact some esoteric piece of economic policy will make little difference to voters.'

'When the whole of Western Europe is overrun by Putin's army and we're all the slaves of Russian oligarchy,' said one anonymous No campaigner, 'what then for this so-called Norwegian oil fund?'

Insiders believe that the character Harry Stamper, played by Bruce Willis in the hit movie *Armageddon*, was based on Professor McGavin.

Other Referendum News From The Past Week

Friday 9 May

Labour leader, Ed Miliband, once again found his way north today, to make a speech in Dundee in which he promised that Scotland would 'never have had it so good' if they vote No to independence in September, and then elect a Labour government to Westminster next May. Ignoring the fact that virtually no one in the entire kingdom can imagine him leading anything, never mind a country of 63 million people, Mr Miliband pressed ahead for all the world like there wasn't going to be a majority Conservative government in the UK next year.

Clutching a teddy bear and speaking without notes, Mr Miliband outlined a five-point plan for the future of Scotland within the UK. In the event of a No vote/Labour government combination, he promised Holyrood would have a new contract with the rest of the UK that would guarantee:

- Scotland full ownership of Andy Murray, year round, bar the two weeks of Wimbledon
- the right to dispose of Trident, as Scotland sees fit, to the highest bidder
- Scottish women the right to sleep with a Ewan McGregor, James McAvoy or Gerard Butler of their choice
- a new public holiday on 8 April, The Witch Is Dead Day, when every man, woman and child in

Scotland will have the right to beat a Tory with a heavy wooden truncheon

- free stuff, every day, in perpetuity

In response, the friend of a spokesman for the Scottish First Minister, Alex Salmond, said that the people of Scotland would be unimpressed. 'No Labour politician can come up here making completely unrealistic, bold statements about how wonderful and perfect everything's going to be after this vote. That's our job.'

Dr Ian Shackleton is unsure whether Mr Miliband's approach will work. 'For sure, technically when you're leader of one of the UK's two biggest parties, it increases your chances of becoming Prime Minister. But seriously? Ed Miliband? Prime Minister? No one wants that. No one.'

There was further uncertain news for supporters of the Union, when it was revealed the Big Gordon Brown was due to head north for the summer to front up the No campaign. Big Gordon is scheduled to appear in a series of events across the nation, culminating in a one man Chippendales act at the King's Theatre in Glasgow in September.

Wednesday 7 May

Excitement swept through Scotland today like a virulent syphilitic infection, when news leaked that Prime Minister, David Cameron, is to take a more active part in the Referendum campaign once the Conservative Party Euro election disaster has been dealt with.

With the UK's economy bounding ahead, the housing market exploding back to pre-credit crunch levels, optimism raging for England's forthcoming World Cup triumph and the banks experiencing an incredible boom time (albeit, no one's told him that it's food banks), the PM is on a roll, and feels confident in heading north to embrace the campaign.

'This is what the No campaign have been waiting for,' said Dr Shackleton. 'Better Together has been an unmitigated disaster. Directionless, feckless, clueless and leaderless. They need a great political mind to step into the breach. In the absence of one, the Prime Minister will have to do.'

News broke in the *Herald* this morning that a friend of an insider on the staff of a senior assistant to a source in Labour had referred to the PM as being 'toxic' in Scotland. Nevertheless, while acknowledging that the quote was genuine, senior aides to the PM argued that it had not been meant in the pejorative.

'People in Scotland love David Cameron,' said an unidentified Tory spokesperson, 'they just don't know it yet.' He confirmed that the PM will undertake a series of major events in Scotland in the lead-up to the Referendum, putting him in touch with ordinary people, and spreading his appeal across a wide spectrum of the voting public, including:

- breakfast with the Queen at Balmoral
- an audience with Billy Connolly

- a pub crawl in Glasgow finishing at the Tolbooth at 7.30 a.m.
- making a speech to a cheering audience of thousands at the Commonwealth Games
- wrestling a stag bare-chested

Insiders believe that Mr Cameron and his family will rent a one-up, one-down in Cumbernauld for the duration of the summer so that he can be closer to the action.

I asked Dr Shackleton if he thought the Prime Minister would resign if it turned out that Scotland was lost to the Union on his watch.

'Resign?' said Shackleton. 'No. Invade maybe. But not resign.'

19 May 2014

Salmond Lays Claim To Falkland Islands, Gibraltar And Other British OTs

The war of words over Scottish independence increased this morning, with Alex Salmond stating that Scotland would look to claim its rightful percentage of the remnants of the Empire Formerly Known as British following a Yes vote in September's Referendum. There are currently fourteen British Overseas Territories, including Bermuda, Pitcairn Islands and the Falklands Islands (officially known in Scotland as the Archie Gemmill Archipelago).

'If they want us to take our percentage of the debt,' said Mr Salmond, talking to veteran interviewer John Humphrys on Radio 4's *Today* programme, 'then we want our percentage of the colonies. Whether we take, for example, the entire Cayman Islands, or whether we take a beach in Montserrat here and an ice sheet on Antarctica there, remains to be seen.'

An insider claimed that a friend of an unnamed Westminster source stated that if Salmond wanted to argue over islands, then Shetland, Orkney and Cumbrae were on the agenda.

In what many analysts are seeing as a ramping up of tension, news channels were reporting that the one ship the Royal Navy has left was seen on 'routine' manoeuvres off the coast of Millport as recently as yesterday morning, with some reports suggesting that the Ritz Café was fired upon in a disagreement over the price of a double 99.

'The ownership of islands has been disputatious throughout human civilisation,' says Dr Ian Shackleton of the Glasgow School of Politics and Football, 'and you just need to look at what's happening now in the South China Sea to see the dangers involved and the potential for conflict.'

Speaking to me this morning from his office on the 98th floor of the splendid new Burj Caledonia at the heart of Glasgow's Spice District, Dr Shackleton was in contemplative mood. Sipping his third cappuccino of the morning, while looking out over the golden turrets of the city, he continued, 'Usually it's not about the islands themselves, of course, but about oil and mineral rights in the surrounding area. In this case, however, it's clear that the SNP are after a decent beach where the water doesn't shrink your testicles to total invisibility, and there are no midgies.'

Some political insiders believe that the SNP are seeking finally to repair the damage of the Darien fiasco of the 1690s, which saw Scotland's previous bid to become a world power scuppered by disease, famine, English duplicity and attack from the Spanish. Others have suggested that downright, f***witted stupidity played its part.

'It's a trade war, and this time Scotland thinks it's in a better position,' says Shackleton. 'Everyone hates England now. Just look at Hollywood movies, and Eurovision. Salmond sees this as his chance to start the new Scottish Empire, that will one day rule the world.'

Insiders believe that plans are already afoot to open the first Scotmid on Antarctica, selling chips, IrnBru and Tunnock's tea cakes.

Other Referendum News From The Past Week

Friday 16 May

The Referendum debate was thrown into crisis today with the declaration by the House of Lords constitution committee that if the Scottish government seriously thought they would be completely independent by 24 March 2016 following a Yes vote, 'they could prepare to get their arse handed to them.'

House of Lords experts reported that it was the strongest language used by one of the chamber's committees since the start of the Opium Wars in 1839.

Chair of the committee, Baroness Finklestein of Shepton Mallet, stated that the rest of the UK could not just lie down and be dictated to by the government in Scotland and that, 'if it means we employ our usual negotiating tactic by bombing the crap out of Edinburgh, so be it.'

A spokesperson for the SNP reacted stoutly by stating that the House of Lords itself was 'an unconstitutional, unelected piece of geriatric pish,' and that they'd be writing a strongly worded letter on the subject to a variety of media outlets.

Analysts have described the exchange as a presage to war, with many fully expecting total armed revolt, bloodshed and many millions dead by the end of the year.

'Countries don't just vote for independence and off they go to the Hundred Acre Wood to live a happy life, devoid of struggle,' says Dr Shackleton. 'Countries are born out of war, terror, endless struggle, death and the occasional baffling offside decision. Let no man be mistaken; war is coming. And it won't be one of those nice wars you saw in a 1950s movie. Ice cream will be spilled, make no mistake.'

Other political analysts believe that Shackleton was using ice cream as a metaphor.

It is believed that both Westminster and Holyrood have sent constitutional experts to South Sudan in recent weeks to get tips on how to successfully break a country apart.

Wednesday 14 May

Despite continuing outrage from voters in Scotland that a poll paid for by the Cabinet Office Devolution Team has been buried, Westminster today again refused to reveal the poll's findings, leaving many to speculate that it shows support for the Union plummeting into a rancid, rat-infected abyss.

The poll by Ipsos MORI and paid for with money personally wrenched from the hands of starving Scottish children by millionaire, Eton-educated cabinet ministers, has begun to trend worldwide on social media, as the planet is gripped by the Scottish independence question.

As a sop to voters, analysts and crazy people on the Internet, the Cabinet Office this morning released a poll of what people think the Buried Poll is about.

- 51% think it shows the Yes vote soaring to at least 15 points higher than No
- 17% think it shows that Scottish people consider David Cameron to be a dick
- 16% believe there is no poll and that someone, somewhere is just making shit up
- 15% believe the poll shows Westminster is preparing the case that iScotland will need to be known as the Former United Caledonian Kingdom (F***) Scotland
- 1% think the Cabinet Office are refusing to release the poll out of modesty as it shows the Yes vote flatlining

Political analysts, such as Dr Shackleton, believe that the #PublishThePoll fiasco is causing nothing but damage for Better Together. 'It's been a total train wreck of a week for them. First we learn that Alistair Darling hasn't just been dropped from the Better Together team, but that he's been banished from the land and lent out on loan to the Government of Ukraine, and now this. This is a classic case of something minor – and remember, no matter its results, today's poll is tomorrow's cut-price ticket on a week-old chicken in Lidl – growing exponentially, entirely down to stupidity.'

Another poll in this morning's newspapers reveals that voters believe that there will be no end to the stupidity, regardless of the outcome of the vote.

26 May 2014

Rumours Of SNP-UKIP Alliance Sweep Westminster

A secret Holyrood memo has revealed that shock discussions have taken place between the SNP and European earthquake specialists, UKIP, with a view to forming an unlikely alliance at next year's Westminster General Election, regardless of the outcome of the independence vote. Prince Charles immediately compared it to the Molotov-Ribbentrop pact that divvied up Eastern Europe before the start of World War II.

Political insiders believe that while the two parties might seem natural antagonists, they are joined by their feeling of alienation from Westminster and a shared vision of shaking up the system. In the event of a No vote, they will work together towards Westminster granting Scotland another Referendum within five years. Should there be a Yes vote, the SNP would agree not to launch their expected insurrection to take back Berwick and the land around Carlisle, with UKIP agreeing to move Trident into English waters within the time it takes to float a nuclear submarine down the west coast.

'As Heroclidius once said,' says Dr Ian Shackleton of the Glasgow School of Politics and Football, 'the enemy of my enemy's enemy is my friend's enemy. Both the SNP and UKIP dislike Westminster and they both rage against the traditional establishment. UKIP hate everyone except the English, while the SNP like everyone except the English, so in that sense by joining together they complete the circle. Yes, it's as uneasy an alliance as that between men and elves, but they'll still fancy their chances of taking down the walls of Mordor.'

Sensing the possibility of unrest amongst its grassroots support, the SNP leadership were quick to distance themselves from the rumours of this new political axis. 'UKIP are a party of reactionary, pie-eating, spunk-muppets, and we in the SNP do not break bread with such people,' said the friend of an unidentified party spokesperson.

Nigel Farage was unavailable for comment this morning as he was too busy spending time with ordinary people, downing flagons of finest ale for breakfast.

Dr Shackleton, however, is unsure of the likely benefits of the Union, if it exists, for either party. 'What we're seeing with UKIP now,' he told me this morning, as we talked in his office on the 98th floor of the colossal Demetrius the Cynic Building at the heart of Glasgow's Latin Quarter, 'is a replica of the whole SDP brouhaha of the early '80s. Remember how that was going to change British politics? With Westminster's first past the post system, it would take a massive swing in any individual constituency for UKIP to win even a single seat. Perhaps Farage might get into Parliament, if he picks the right borough and has a pint individually with every voter between now and next May – and, of course, if those voters don't think he's a dick, and he doesn't die of alcohol poisoning – but that's it. Remember, today's earthquake is tomorrow's cholera epidemic. Essentially UKIP is a one-man vanity project.'

Suggestions from Labour and the Conservatives that therein lies the true similarity between the SNP and UKIP, immediately resulted in the re-appearance of Nicola Sturgeon's nippy sweetie face on the campaign trail.

Other Referendum News From The Past Week

Wednesday 21 May

There was major headline news yesterday when the General Assembly of the Church of Scotland said something about the independence debate, although no one really paid that much attention, thereby rendering the major headline news instantly obsolete.

Addressing the Assembly in a kiosk at the far end of Portobello beach, Labour's Shadow Foreign Minister, Douglas Alexander – the last remaining member of the Church of Scotland under fifty – put the case for Scotland's Union with the rest of the United Kingdom, while a church minister of no fixed name stated that Scotland ought to be independent. Since members of the Church of Scotland have vowed to be nice to each other for all of space/time, the other five attendees of the

General Assembly then agreed to disagree and shook hands over a cucumber sandwich.

The Church of Scotland ran into unexpected controversy last week when it stated it would hold a service of reconciliation three days after September's vote, regardless of the result. Many friends of political analysts thought the move condescending, others said that they were looking forward to the fight and that they would never speak to (insert *Yes* or *No*)-voting scum ever again, while an unidentified spokesperson for the Catholic Church issued a statement saying, 'Who gave those entitled, pompous w****** the monopoly on reconciliation?'

'These are tough times for the Church of Scotland,' says Dr Shackleton. 'Yes, the old are dying and not being replaced, and they're shedding members by the bucketload over the issue of gay ministers. But at the heart of it lies their central message; let's all be nice to each other. Seriously, it's just so five hundred years ago. No one's nice to anyone anymore. We're a nation of sociopathic, money-grabbing, YouTube-posting, Buckfast junkies, with a life expectancy of 57.'

A spokesperson for the Church passed away before he could reply to Dr Shackleton's comments.

'Some might say I'm being harsh,' continued Shackleton, 'but have you heard one ounce of humility or decency in this campaign? Have you heard one person say, "actually my opponent makes a good point, that's one thing we'll miss if we get our way"? Sneering, carping, petty point-scoring from both sides. Doesn't it just depress the crap out of you? Bugger this, I'm going for a doughnut.'

Later the Church of Scotland announced that it had done a deal with Burger King to give away free Double Whoppers with every baptism.

Saturday 24 May

A vision of Scotland covered in giant wind turbines, all of which stand idle, as barely a zephyr of wind crosses the country, was presented this morning, but it wasn't a page from science fiction. The findings come from a new report by scientists at the Glasgow Institute of Special Science, which found that the amount of wind blowing across Scotland has reduced every year since 1993, with only one minor increase in 2001. The paper, published in *British Scientist Monthly*, predicts that Scotland will be completely free of wind in just over five years, and that the £267 billion so far invested in wind farms will have been wasted.

'We all knew climate change would be devastating,' said Professor Malcolm Connery of the GISS, 'but our report shows just how destructive it can be. With weather patterns changing around the globe, it looks like the winds blowing across the Atlantic will head further south. Our extensive scientific modelling indicates that the north Atlantic will soon be completely still for an extended period, possibly lasting upwards of five or six thousand years. It's unlikely that Scotland will see any wind much after spring 2019. It doesn't look good for the north of England either.'

Alistair Darling, lead scaremonger for Better Together said, 'This leaves the entire edifice of the Yes campaign in tatters. Vote Yes and we all die in poverty, it's as simple as that.'

With no winds to blow weather systems across the nation, climatologists predict Scotland's weather will stay the same as it is on the day the last winds blow, predicted to be 13 May 2019, for all time.

'You'd better hope the sun's shining,' said Professor Connery, 'but then, if it is, it'll never change, there'll be no wind to cool the air, and Scotland will turn into Western Sahara. Good luck with that.'

Political analysts, such as Dr Shackleton, are in no doubt the devastating effect the report will have on the SNP and the campaign for an independent Scotland. 'Alex Salmond has invested everything in green energy, with wind at the forefront. If we become independent and then the wind stops blowing, where will we be? Bankrupt, and literally powerless. With rUK looking on, and more than likely laughing, Scotland would be forced to look east. Putin would move in, and before you know it, Scotland would become just another beleaguered state of the Russian Federation.'

As we sat in his 98th floor office, the mood darkened and Shackleton finally cracked open the bottle of sixty year-old Macallan that he'd been saving for the end of times.

'With the Russians on England's doorstep, war is inevitable. For God's sake, let us sit upon the ground and tell sad stories of the death of kingdoms.'

The ice clinked in the glass, as dark clouds approached the city, moving ever so slowly on a breath of wind.

2 June 2014

Salmond Steps Up To The Plate For Blockbuster Summer

Love him or loathe him, voters in Scotland must prepare themselves to see far more of SNP über-leader Alex Salmond over the summer, as Yes campaign strategists look to make the most of what they see as one of the clear advantages they have over Better Together. While the No campaign is fragmented and frequently fractured, with the likes of Big Gordon Brown and David Cameron forced onto the same platform, resulting in an often-mixed message, the Yes campaign has been far more focused, largely because of the guiding influence of the First Minister.

Political analysts, such as Dr Ian Shackleton of the Glasgow School of Politics and Football, are in no doubt that we'll be seeing more and more of the SNP leader as the weeks go on. 'It's a bold and clever strategy,' he told me this morning, as we spoke in his 98th floor office in the magnificent new Blair The Deceiver Building at the heart of Glasgow's Persian Rug District. 'Sure, this vote is about the next thousand years, not what happens in 2016. Truly, it's not about economics, it's not about welfare policy, it's not about Jeremy Paxman. It's about much more existential stuff than that. Nevertheless, at the heart of it, it's about voters, and what do voters see? On one side, Alex Salmond, a man of the people. On the other, David Cameron, a man of the trough. Everyone in Scotland, even that posh bloke you heard talking in a wine bar once who voted Conservative, thinks Cameron is the bastard son of Lord Voldemort and a jackal.'

Now, as they go for the jugular and try to push home Salmond's popular appeal, the Yes campaign intend throwing the First Minister into a variety of manly situations to exacerbate the differences between him and the bullying, effete, Westminster Nancy boy.

The next few weeks will see Salmond:

- swim from Aberdeen to Hammerfest
- wrestle Yang Guang, the male panda at Edinburgh zoo, wearing nothing but a pair of Speedos
- kill Piers Morgan with his bare hands
- shoot things
- lead the Black Watch on an incursion south of the border to retake Berwick
- appear naked in a Cosmopolitan centrefold
- take the ring of power deep into the heart of Mordor and throw it into Mount Doom

'Women will go wild for him,' says Shackleton, 'and men are going to look up to his movie star charisma. It's going to be like watching *Braveheart II*.'

Holyrood insiders say that the SNP have been looking east, to leader of the Russian Federation, Vladimir Putin, for inspiration. 'Watching that guy,' said one friend of a friend of a political insider, 'is like watching all those Robbie Williams videos from back in the day. You know, he'd be a cowboy for one song, then a spy, then a racing car driver, and so on. That's what Putin's like. Of course, he has nuclear weapons, so it's a bit scarier, but Mr Salmond needs to copy him. People will go balls out for it.'

Rumours around Holyrood also suggest that the First Minister will officially change his name to The Incredible Captain Scotland in order to accentuate his manliness.

Other Referendum News From The Past Week

Wednesday 28 May

The Referendum debate reached new levels of petty name-calling, squabbling, sophistry, fibbery and incompetence today with both sides presenting financial figures on the immediate benefits to individuals in the year following independence. The claim and counter-claim continued most of the day, leaving voters asleep in their chairs. There were reports in central Glasgow that upwards of seventeen people were literally bored to death while watching the news. Another nine were said to have been treated in hospital for infectious verbal diarrhoea inhalation.

Better Together promised that if the nation voted No in September's vote:

- each individual would get a Ferrari and a voucher for free sex or chocolate
- Placing their own valuation on independence, the SNP announced that in the event of a Yes vote:
- the grass would be greener

Following the announcements, the two sides proceeded to rubbish the opposition claims, until finally Danny Alexander and Alex Salmond agreed to meet in a 15-round naked cock-wrestling match in Glasgow's George Square.

Political analysts, such as Dr Shackleton, are unimpressed with the latest bullshit. 'It's like watching the crappiest, most mind-numbing, face-palm of a game of football you ever saw, but you don't get to leave early or go home after ninety minutes,' he told me this morning, as we talked over a moccachino 'There are still over three months to go, and they're going to spend all that time stuck in midfield, kicking each other. Oh, for a defence-splitting pass...'

Friends of party political insiders doubt that there's a defence-splitting pass to be had, from either side. With politicians repeatedly saying the same stuff over and over, statistics and costs and money and figures being tossed around like a baby in a wind tunnel, and with one day lurching inexorably into the next on the back of the same old shit, Dr Shackleton believes voters can look ahead to little other than what's gone before.

'I'll say it again,' he said, looking out over the golden spires of the city. 'It's not about economics. A bountiful country can be badly run, a country low in resources can be well run. This is about something much more intrinsic. These politicians should be having big and bold discussions about our place in the world, and in these isles. Instead they squabble over the price of a deep-fried Tunnock's Tea Cake.'

Late news reports indicated that the Salmond/Alexander cock-wrestling match had gone to extra time and penalties.

Friday 30 May

There was rejoicing in Scotland today as the formal sixteen-week Referendum campaign finally got under way. 'Thank God,' said one ordinary voter this morning, 'maybe now politicians, and people on the Internet, will feel free to speak their minds.'

Tricia Marwick, presiding officer of the Scottish Parliament, marked the start of the regulated period of the campaign by saying that she thought the sides would be able to 'come together' after the vote, regardless of the outcome. Later, however, she clarified her comments by stating that she meant they'd come together in the way that Rangers and Celtic fans came together after the 1980 Scottish Cup Final.

Other ordinary people from ordinary hardworking families, admitted that they were already suffocating beneath the weight of spurious and disingenuous bullshit, and that the sixteen-week period seemed like an esoteric triviality, nothing more than an excuse for politicians to talk even more than they already had been doing. Addressing such ordinary people, the Scottish Parliament issued a statement outlining the specific rules that governed the last three and a half months of the campaign. The statement confirmed that there would be limits on:

- spending

The statement also confirmed that there would be no limits on:

- politicians making stuff up
- outrage at perceived bias of the BBC
- comparing iScotland to South Sudan, North Korea and Somalia
- use of the term 'democratic deficit'
- Big Gordon Brown turning up on your doorstep, smiling

Dr Ian Shackleton is relieved that the campaign can get down to serious business. 'The board is set, the pieces are moving. We come to it at last, the great political debate of our time. The weeks ahead promise so much.

There's the Salmond-Cameron best-of-seven Flappy Bird play-off, we'll get to see Danny Alexander's head literally explode live on national television, there's the metaphorical Scottish Parliament wet T-shirt competition and, of course, there's the serious, in-depth debate about Scotland's place in the world and the opportunities presented by both a Yes and a No vote.'

Later, Dr Shackleton admitted that none of the above would actually happen.

9 June 2014

Better Together Look To Scoop Awards

In exciting news for Better Together, unnamed political pundits this week said that there was every possibility that the team behind Scotland's No Vote for September's Referendum could be winners of the forthcoming *Citizen Kane Economic Digest* Worst Political Campaign Of All Time award.

'We're certainly doing everything in our power to make this the most disastrous political campaign that anyone has ever seen,' said Alistair Darling, Better Together's über-chief. 'Just when you think it can't get any worse, we think of new ways of plumbing the depths and sending confirmed No voters over to the other side. The SNP say that to achieve our true potential as a nation we need to be independent. We, at Better Together, are demonstrating true levels of greatness – in the field of political ineptitude – from a cross border perspective.'

Although many seasoned observers, and friends of seasoned observers, had presumed that Better Together would struggle to get much worse than they'd already been, this week they brought out the big guns and showed those observers who's the boss. In a little more than 72 hours:

- Darling caused uproar by accusing Alex Salmond of being the bastard child from the Satanic union of Kim Jong-Il and Eva Braun
- The UK Treasury produced a document entitled *Patronising Guide For Fat Scottish Pie-Junkies*, giving step-by-step instructions on how to waste money, with the well-known L'Oréal strapline, slightly amended to: "Because you're stupid."
- Prime Minister David Cameron coerced President Obama into denouncing Scottish independence, with threats of a full-scale British invasion of the eastern seaboard of the United States
- The campaign continued to roll out a never ending troupe of scientists, political grandees and John Reid to issue dire warnings on just how catastrophically shit everything's going to be in Scotland should there be a Yes vote
- Darling defended the No campaign booklet, *Your Baby Could Die Between The Jaws Of A Zombie Nationalist*, as presenting a positive message for the future of the UK

'When the dust has settled on the campaign,' said Dr Ian Shackleton of the Glasgow School of Politics and Football, when we spoke this morning, 'and the bodies of the damned are being shovelled into the council skip of unrecyclable, contaminated waste, this will be remembered, and taught in political classrooms for generations to come, as how not to run a campaign. Imagine Fred Goodwin, the captain of the *Titanic*, the guy in charge of health and safety at Chernobyl and one of the Muppets had got together to run a political campaign, then multiply it by Scotland versus Peru in '78, and you might get close to how atrocious this has been.'

With only a hundred days to go before the vote, Big Gordon Brown is expected to attempt to make matters even worse for Better Together by joining the campaign full time. In a speech this morning to a group of babies in Dundee he will tell them, 'Alex Salmond's ego is writing cheques his country can't cash.'

Other Referendum News From The Past Week

Friday 6 June

A shock internal US Department of Defense report has revealed secret plans for an invasion of Scotland. Sources close to unidentified officials in the department have confirmed that President Obama has ratified the report's findings, which would be implemented in the event of a Yes vote in September's Referendum, and should David Cameron ask for US assistance in crushing the rebellious Scots. Illustrated with photographs of Lego figures storming across the border using the latest US military hardware, its writers predict that the Scots could be overwhelmed quickly, and that any fighting would be 'over by Christmas'.

The report quotes US intelligence sources as comparing SNP leader, Alex Salmond, to former North Korean despot Kim Jong-Il, saying that he has the same determination to turn Scotland into a rogue state, with four million land mines laid across the border with England, and no food. DoD insiders contend that any invasion should happen quickly, before the Scots become too entrenched in their isolation. Further to this, the report states that any Scottish forces would be easily overcome as it is 'a nation of deep-fried-Irn-Bru-eating alcoholic drug addicts who would kill their own grandmother for a pie and Bovril.'

An SNP spokesperson denied that you could deep fry IrnBru.

When asked about American invasion plans for Scotland, President Obama seemed to verify the reports when he said, 'I'll admit it. London came along with us when we crushed Iraq, the least we can do is repay the debt. So, if we have to, we'll crush Scotland. We crushed them before, when we beat them 5–1 in Florida in 2012, and we can crush them again. I'm a man of my word. I said when I first ran for this office that I'd close down Guantanamo Bay, and now, here I am, six years later, just letting everybody outta there. Scotland beware.'

It is believed that the invasion would start with the Americans securing the strategic port of Millport. The Scottish government are thought to be considering strengthening their forces in the Millport area as a precaution.

SNP deputy leader, Nicola Sturgeon, said, 'He pulls a gun, you pull a knife. He puts one of your men in the hospital, you glass the bastard with a broken bottle. That's the Glasgow way.'

Wednesday 4 June

The Institute for Fiscal Studies today revised its economic forecast for an independent Scotland. A statement issued on behalf of the IFS began:

'iScotland would be completely and utterly f*****, right from the off. We're looking at a South Sudan type situation here. If you're thinking of voting for independence, you're a newbie simpleton. Forget it. I mean seriously, everybody's going to die if this happens. Fly, you fools! Or just vote no, and that'll save you having to fly in the first place.'

In a dual announcement, easyJet said that in the event of a Yes vote, they would lay on more flights from Glasgow, Edinburgh, Inverness and Aberdeen for the 19 September.

A Better Together spokesperson immediately hailed the findings of the IFS report, pointing to its integrity, honesty, and non-partisan wording. Meanwhile, Yes campaign supporters marched in an orderly procession upon the headquarters of the IFS, carrying torches and pitchforks.

'Better Together just can't help themselves,' said Dr Shackleton. 'They insist that they'll be more positive, then some group or other produces a negative report based on UK government figures, and Alistair Darling can't say 'see, I told you it'd be shit' quickly enough.'

While the Yes campaign have routinely based financial projections for iScotland on the price of oil being \$700/ barrel for the next 50 years, the No campaign have used estimates which suggest barrels of oil will be going 2-for-1 in Lidl for 99p.

'The truth as ever,' said Shackleton, as he looked out over the golden spires of Glasgow from his 98th floor office in the new Ally McLeod Complex at the heart of the city's Latin American Quarter, 'lies crushed and broken beneath the weight of mendacity and misrepresentation.'

Politicians, news programmes, political analysts, and friends of political analysts, have agreed to suspend the discussion on Scottish independence until after the summer to give everyone a break.

16 June 2014

Millport To Go It Alone
In New Independence Shock

The movement of the polls may be going only one way, with the Yes campaign on a roll and Better Together lurching from one inadequate catchphrase to the next, but this weekend was not all good news for Alex Salmond.

In a new blow to the First Minister's assertions that life will be business as usual – only better – following a Yes vote in September's Referendum, officials in Millport on the island of Great Cumbrae have indicated that if Scotland secedes from the Union, and the country takes its place in the world order as the Former United Caledonian Kingdom of Scotland, Millport is likely to seek independence for itself. While some commentators and political analysts are sceptical of Millport's chances of going it alone, others point to the fact that Millport is rich in natural resources – such as fish suppers, rock and cycle hire – and is well suited to become the Liechtenstein of the west.

'Globally, we are in an era of national fragmentation, and Mr Salmond would be unwise to ignore the signs,' says Dr Ian Shackleton of the Glasgow School of Politics and Football. As we sit in his office on the 98th floor of the spectacular new Buckfast Building, overlooking the city's Alcohol Quarter, Dr Shackleton is in expansive mood. 'There are all sorts of rumours coming out of Millport. They're looking at off-shore banking, they're talking to the Russians about building a submarine base, there's talk of them transforming the Ritz Café into a $247m casino, and there's even suggestions that they might try and attract the curling stone trade away from Ailsa Craig. F*** Scotland better watch its back.'

With speculation mounting amongst pundits, politicians, political insiders and friends of political insiders, newspapers today are reporting that plans are already afoot for Millport to place itself firmly on the map with several statement events in the coming eighteen months:

- Great Cumbrae to host the next series of Bear Gryll's *The Island*
- the launch of a new T20 tournament, the Great Cumbrae Premier League (GCPL), with teams in Kames Bay, Keppel Pier, Fintray Bay and Crocodile Rock
- Millport to make a late bid to host the 2022 Winter Olympics
- the Ritz Café to sell half-price 99's
- the launch of the Millport To Mars exploratory two-man space expedition, with a couple of guys from down the Kelburne

Garrett Carmichael, the Millport-based lawyer at the vanguard of the breakaway movement, was in bullish mood as she made an unscheduled appearance on *Newsround*. 'There's a hubris about the SNP that we've seen before. From the Darien Scheme to Argentina '78, all the way to Glasgow Rangers and the RBS, the Scots have a way of taking something bold or successful and making a complete arse of it. Why is this going to be any different? That's why Millport will be better off breaking away. Tax revenue from Mapes joke shop alone will see iMillport's GDP nearly double that of iScotland by 2034. One day soon North Sea oil will run out, but fart cushions and itching powder are forever.'

In other related news, Millport Football Association have placed an injunction in the courts in an attempt to replace Scotland in Euro 2016 qualifying.

Other Referendum News From The Past Week

Saturday 14 June

The Better Together campaign was reeling again this morning as it awoke to find that it had lost further territory overnight to the Insurgent Cybernats for an Independent Scotland (ICIS). ICIS, a radical online movement, has made huge gains across the whole of Scotland, swallowing up entire towns and cities as Better Together crumbles before the onslaught.

The leadership structure and funding of ICIS is not entirely understood, but while some have claimed that the campaign has been orchestrated from the office of the First Minister, Alex Salmond has been quick to distance himself from all Cybernat activity.

'Clearly the Better Together people have been very poorly prepared,' said Dr Shackleton. 'Westminster thought they'd done a good job, they thought they'd provided them with everything they needed to fight the campaign and yet they just folded overnight.'

To make matters worse for Better Together, it appears that ICIS have been taking the opposition's weapons and ammunition and using it against them.

'Better Together just fled, leaving behind all this crap,' said Shackleton, 'and ICIS have been using it all. Every leaflet, every hand-out, every press announcement, every statement uttered by Alistair Darling and his minions has been turned against BT and they're in total meltdown.'

As the international community looks on in helpless disbelief, various world leaders from the Pope to President Obama, not to mention people who don't lead anything such as Hillary Clinton, have expressed support for Better Together. Nevertheless, whether these words of support ultimately lead to putting more grassroots people on the ground to fight the ICIS insurgency remains to be seen.

Yet, Dr Shackleton has a word of caution for all involved in the Referendum debate. Stroking his long white beard, as he looked out over the golden spires of the city, he said, 'Be on your guard. There are older and fouler things than Cybernats in the deep places of the world.'

Thursday 12 June 2014

In what many analysts consider to be a breakthrough moment in the campaign, both sides today demanded that their opponent apologise for things that hadn't yet been said. As the tone of the debate inevitably slides from the gutter into the sewer (with descent into the sorrowful inferno of the fiery abyss expected some time in the middle of August), apologies are being demanded, issued, rejected and rephrased on a daily basis.

A new poll this morning shows that more people are disgusted with something or other than at any time since voters started to become disgusted in the early 1990s, and in the last three days a record thirty-seven apologies were issued in relation to #indyref, up thirty-seven from this time last year.

'This is largely down to people being dicks,' says Dr Shackleton. 'However, it's not as though we can expect that to change any time soon.'

Now, with temperatures rising and words spewing forth like toxic lava, both the Yes and No campaigns are demanding apologies in advance.

'It's inevitable that Alistair Darling is going to make some new, egregious claim about something stupid,' said an unidentified friend of a Yes spokesperson. 'We demand that he apologise now for everything he intends saying over the next three months. He should be ashamed.'

An aide to the friend of a No vote insider responded, 'These things that are going to be said by the Yes campaign are a total disgrace. It starts at the top. Alex Salmond waves a flag and the next thing you know someone on Twitter is making nasty, pejorative claims about JK Rowling, suggesting she can't write for biscuits. Or worse. It's time they apologised. For everything.'

In a later development, Yes insiders denied that they'd said what they were going to say and demanded that No insiders apologise for demanding an apology.

Shortly afterwards Scotland exploded.

23 June 2014

Hunt For #Indyref Smoking Gun Heats Up

With the final few months of the battle in full swing, both the Yes and No campaigns are looking for the big breakthrough that would clinch what is becoming, in the eyes of a majority of political analysts, a fascinatingly tight race. And while solid political argument and well-researched statistics, allied with surreptitiously funded propaganda and scaremongering, can effect a shift in the polls over time, nothing creates greater movement than a scandal, or the political nirvana of the smoking gun.

Consequently, as the longest day of the year is left behind, and the first hint of autumn starts to sweep, wringwraith-like across the blighted Scottish hills on the cold winds of eternal damnation, both campaigns are reported to be running covert ops in the hope of uncovering what could be the killer blow in the struggle for Scotland's future.

'The trouble is,' says Dr Ian Shackleton, of the Glasgow School of

Politics and Football, 'there's nothing out there. There are no selfies of Alex Salmond's privates, there's no Westminster secret invasion plan, there's unlikely at this stage even to be a Chris Christie-esque Bridgegate scandal.'

Instead, says Dr Shackleton, the teams leading the campaigns have given their covert operatives a Scandal Wish List (SWL), with orders to go out and find evidence of the scandals whether they exist or not. Shackleton claims that moles on either side passed him the lists, which point clearly to the mindset of those involved and to the potential rumourmongering that the summer holds.

The No campaign SWL is known to be seven pages long, with the following highlights:

- pictures of Alex Salmond and Nicola Sturgeon walking out of a hotel room hand in hand, with her pants on his head
- an SNP memo outlining plans to ethnically cleanse Scotland of all English within six months of independence
- proof that Salmond is aiming to join Warsaw Pact II
- details of Scottish government plans to enter into a currency union with Mordor
- official Scottish government North Sea energy estimates, predicting that the oil will run out by quarter past four on the 21 September this year

Despite the acknowledged fact that none of these items actually exist, a No campaign spokesman was outraged. 'One does not simply walk into a currency union with Mordor,' he told the BBC.

The Yes campaign wish list is thought to be slightly longer, with the highlights including:

- proof of Westminster plans to turn Scotland into a dump for nuclear waste
- photographs of Alistair Darling being debagged and radished by an unholy alliance of David Cameron, Gordon Brown and Rolf Harris
- details of a Westminster government bill to rename Scotland as Thatcherland Minor, with a seven hundred foot high statue of Lady Thatcher erected in George Square
- copies of a No campaign 'begging e-mail' to every world leader, celebrity and author of wizard fiction pleading for their backing

Despite the recognised non-existence of any of these items, Yes campaigners are infuriated. 'This is the kind of weasel-worded wankery that we've come to expect from the likes of David Cameron and his bitch, Darling,' said one unidentified friend of a Yes campaign insider.

Stroking his long white beard as he looked out over the golden spires of the city, from his 98th floor office in the newly renovated Archie Gemmill Building at the heart of Glasgow's Football Quarter, Dr Shackleton was in contemplative mood. 'Politicians, pundits and crazy people on the Internet see that little more is to be gained from reasoned argument. The time for measured debate is over. War is coming. Or, at any rate, shouting is coming.'

Other Referendum News From The Past Week

Monday 16 June

As promised in the early spring, Nicola Sturgeon today launched a consultation process over the interim Scottish Constitution, a document that will show the way ahead for Scotland, steering it through the processes between a Yes vote in September and full independence in March 2016, leading to a full written constitution for the independent nation.

'It's disgraceful,' said Ms Sturgeon, speaking to a gathering of Scottish business leaders in the bunker at the 17th of the Old Course at St Andrews, 'that the UK does not have a written constitution. Without such a document, how can a nation even exist? We will eschew the arrogance of the UK approach and look to follow the example of the likes of South Sudan, Iraq and Somalia, all of which have the rights of their citizens enshrined in legally-binding documents.'

Ms Sturgeon announced that the document, entitled Declaration of Arbroath II: Revenge of the Fallen, will be written in the blood of our nation's enemies, and will included such guarantees as:

- everything will be really brilliant for everyone
- there will be no more sadness
- there will be a new Scottish Enlightenment, powered by wind
- Scottish parliamentary sessions will be opened by the Queen, whose speech will begin, 'I'm pure like that, by the way...'
- Trident missiles to be auctioned off on eBay
- Scottish troops to advance on Derby by Christmas
- Scotland will launch a space programme, with the aim of finding new worlds we can beat at football by 2029

'Virtually every country in the world has a written constitution,' says Dr Shackleton, 'so you can understand why the SNP thinks it's important. But let us not forget that tyrants everywhere use their constitution as a smokescreen of legitimacy, and that decent countries with decent governance would still be decent, regardless of the written constitution. Still, it'll give someone somewhere something to do.'

Meanwhile the search for iScotland's Mission Statement, which will serve as the Constitution's tag line, is on. Suggestions so far sent into the SNP's 'Write Scotland's Tagline and Become an Imperial Shekel Millionaire' competition, include:

- I Can't Believe It's Not Norway
- Between Love and Madness Lies Scotland

- Where Buckfast Is A Way Of Life
- Trapped in time. Surrounded by evil. Low on oil.
- Carlsberg don't do countries, but if they did...
- You'd rather be here than in North Korea

'Every country has a mission statement these days,' says Shackleton, 'albeit some of them, such as Greece's 'Making An Arse Of It So You Don't Have To,' are not terribly reassuring.'

30 June 2014

Cameron Considers Moves To Block Yes Vote

Shockwaves were being felt throughout Scotland this morning as press reports indicated the existence of a leaked Downing Street memo which proves that enfeebled Prime Minister, David Cameron, reeling from the conviction of former aide, Andy Coulson, and his chastening defeat at the hands of his European partners, has discussed the possibility of reneging on the Edinburgh Agreement should the vote go in favour of an independent Scotland.

'Cameron looks weak,' said one friend of a source close to an aide to a Conservative party insider. 'His authority is almost gone, and now he's scrabbling around trying to find something to cling to. Scotland's such an easy bet. If they vote for independence, and he says no, it'll make him look strong. The Tories have nothing to lose north of the border anyway, and it'll play well with English voters, who have all come to hate Alex Salmond, even more than they hate Luis Suarez.'

Political commentators believe the move will prove especially successful with women voters hankering after a strong leader. Tory party insiders are believed to be advising the Prime Minister to buff up, so that he looks good in a series of topless beach shots over the summer.

'The guy's going to be hot, and he's going to crush the Scots. People are going to be looking at him and thinking, *Oh my God, what did you eat for breakfast!?* This past week is going to be history.'

The SNP were said to be outraged and disgusted. Reports indicated that Nicola Sturgeon was intending to appear on television looking stern.

'People might think it's a joke,' says Dr Ian Shackleton, of the Glasgow School of Politics and Football, 'but lawyers have argued from the very beginning that the Edinburgh Agreement was a political agreement not a legal one. There is no strict basis in law that would allow Scotland to break free, even if it votes so to do. If it befits the Prime Minister to tell Scotland to jog on, and he's backed by a jingoistic press and a baying population, why should he give Scotland anything?'

Analysts believe that Cameron is also considering achieving his aims by making any conditions on Scottish independence so prescriptively unworkable that they never actually get to break away. These would include:

- as one of the four countries currently making up the UK, Scotland would be required to take on one quarter of the UK national debt, already a number so large it can only be communicated in adjectives
- Scotland would only be entitled to those assets which it held prior to the Act of Union 1707

- Aberdeen would be declared a Free Port, and while rUK might not have access to tax revenue from oil money, neither would iScotland
- the English ambassador to Edinburgh would be able to invoke *jus primae noctis*
- all English landowners in Scotland would be encouraged to populate their land with sheep and send the human population to Canada by boat

As he looks out over the golden spires of the city from his 98th floor office in the newly completed Kris Boyd Tower at the heart of the city's Saxon Quarter, Dr Shackleton is in contemplative mood. Running his fingers through his long, flowing white beard, he added, 'Soon enough, each side will come to regret the touchy-feely, lovefest Clause 30 of the Edinburgh Agreement. All that, let's-be-nice-to-each-other-regardless-of-the-result schtick. Bad things will happen. The world of men will fall, and all will come to darkness.'

Other Referendum News From The Past Week

Friday 27 June

There was another decisive moment in the Referendum

campaign today when Ed Miliband once more defied orders from his mum and headed north to mingle with the rebellious Scots. Accompanied by a crack team of bodyguards, several of whom used to be Ross Kemp, Mr Miliband took to the stage in the coffee shop in Waterstones on Princes Street to wild applause from Chantelle Buffett, 6, and her dad.

Mr Miliband promised that the Scots could be at the forefront of the drive to change Britain, after Labour had won the UK General Election in 2015. The current Labour leader did not make clear, however, who would be Prime Minister in the event of a victory for his party. The notion that Mr Miliband himself might one day lead the country has been widely debunked by virtually everyone on earth. In a recent poll, when asked who they would like to be their next leader, Britons ranked Mr Miliband behind the shoe bomber, one of those ISIS guys currently hacking a path through Iraq, and Sarah Palin. Only Tony Blair, current EU Middle East War Envoy, ranked beneath Mr Miliband in the poll.

'Scotland has always thought big,' said Mr Miliband. 'Stay with us and be part of the most amazing thing that's ever happened ever. Whatever that's going to be.'

Mr Miliband promised the whole of Scotland that if it stuck with the UK, then:

- Britain would rule the world
- everyone in Britain would have their own punkawallah

- women would have flat stomachs and pert boobs
- men would have six-packs and the sexual prowess of a lion
- Scotland would get to replay their game against Uruguay in the 1986 World Cup, although this time without Stevie Nicol

'If you thought this campaign was turning into a Kafkaesque horror show,' says Dr Shackleton, 'you'd be right. It's a recurring nightmare. One side issues a list of promises, which is immediately debunked by their opponents. Shortly afterwards, the other side promises everyone free sex and doughnuts, and the first side splutter into their single malt. There's literally no escape.'

Later Mr Miliband went on a tour of primary schools in the Scottish capital, finally enrolling in a Primary 3 class at St Stephen's School For Boys. His mum said she'd pick him up by quarter past 4.

7 July 2014

Yes Campaign Gets
The World Cup Blues

While the SNP have continued to talk a good game in the ongoing Referendum debate, political analysts are beginning to detect rumblings of frustration and discontent at party headquarters in Narnia. The campaign is now several months removed from the great leap for Yes polling numbers which resulted from Gideon Osborne's insistence that iScotland would be forced to use the Scottish Imperial Shekel rather than the Pound. Despite the campaigning and the rhetoric, and not forgetting the fact that the No campaign has been demonstrably the worst political campaign in living memory anywhere in the world, Yes numbers have, the occasional fluctuation notwithstanding, hit something of a ceiling.

While there have been many reasons given for this apparent slowing down of momentum, including voters tiring of Nicola Sturgeon's stern face telling them off – 'Every time she comes on TV it's like getting a row from your mum,' said one voter – Dr Ian Shackleton, one of the few experts lecturing on politics and football in the country, believes that the sport formerly known as the beautiful game is entirely to blame.

'There's no question the slowing of Yes momentum is as a direct result of the World Cup,' he told me this morning, as we spoke in his office on the 98th floor of the magnificent new Jim Bett Mansions in the city's Icelandic Quarter. 'It's all-consuming, and the SNP have just had to accept that the Referendum campaign, like everything else in the world, has had to play second fiddle.'

While the SNP had been wary of the World Cup from the start, their dream that England would do well, thereby filling the media with stories of English glory and pissing off everyone in Scotland, fell quickly by the wayside on the back of England's complete and utter ineptitude.

'There's no escaping English sporting success in Scotland,' says TV analyst, Professor Malcolm Connery, of the Glasgow Institute of Special Things. 'We share the same national news bulletins, which are of course predominantly aimed at an English audience. When England win stuff, Yes polling numbers go through the roof. But what have we learned from this World Cup? Overseas players clutch their faces, feign injury and, when they can be bothered, look brilliant. English players rarely cheat, looking brilliant is quite beyond them and the only time they clutch their face is in despair when they've just hoofed a corner kick straight into row Z. For the Scots it's been like looking in the mirror.'

With Scotland's arch-rivals gone, it has allowed the country to wallow in the shenanigans, tricks, treats, brilliance and cheating, diving artifice of the rest of the world.

'Those ISIS fellows in Iraq knew the score,' says Shackleton. 'They started taking over towns, and people were just sitting in bars watching the football going, yeah, whatever, blah blah blah, we're watching Ghana versus Germany, bugger off. So they shot the TVs. It wasn't very friendly, but seriously, they had guns, they didn't need to be. Then people were like, oh shit, no football, and there are guys with guns...!'

Rumours that the SNP have been considering sending shock troops into homes and bars around the country to shoot televisions have been strenuously denied. 'The discussions never got past the consultation phase,' said one SNP insider who wished to remain anonymous.

Instead the Yes campaign has been left to wait out the tournament. 'The good news for them,' says Shackleton, 'is that once the World Cup is over there are still two more months to get back in the game. They'll be hoping the Commonwealth Games does for their campaign what the London Olympics did for Boris Johnson.'

The First Minister is believed to be lining up a series of affairs, racist comments and comedic stunts in preparation for his anticipated Boris-bounce.

Other Referendum News From The Past Week

Thursday 3 July

David Cameron once more strode north of the border today, bringing his own homespun brand of folksy, down-to-earth rhetoric to the campaign. Wearing nothing but a kilt, and carrying a claymore soaked in the blood of his enemies strapped across his back, the Prime Minister walked the four hundred and fifty miles to Perth in under three hours, collecting a troupe of ardent supporters along the way.

His speech to a cheering audience of over 70,000 in the grounds of Scone Palace seems set to be a defining moment in the campaign, as voters could be seen visibly turning from Yes to No as he spoke.

'It's what we needed,' said Malky Eight Feet, a publishing executive from Montrose. 'This man's been to Eton, so he knows what he's talking about. Total dude, by the way. Respect.'

Bringing the message that Britain's 'not as shit as you think', and that an independent Scotland would be dining with South Sudan at the aid agency Table of Desperation within months, Mr Cameron urged the 'silent majority of voters' to be heard.

Noting that the phrase 'silent majority' was first used in the 19th century to refer to the dead, critics have claimed that this is proof that the Coalition government are planning electoral fraud on a massive scale. As a result of the speech, Yes campaigners are predicting over two million votes to be cast for No in the name of the deceased.

Deposed Better Together kingpin, Alistair Darling, refused to comment on the allegations, but was seen to raise an eyebrow.

Political analysts, such as Dr Shackleton, are in little doubt that the Prime Minister's increasingly frequent interventions could play a decisive part on the campaign trail.

'Yes, he's condescending,' he told me this morning, 'and the only thing he has in common with your average Scotsman is that he goes bright red in the sun. Yet there's a cumulative effect at work here. These things seep into the subconscious, and the next time you hear the No campaign denouncing him for not caring about Scotland and being too feart to debate the First Minister, there's a small voice reminding you that he walked all the way from Westminster to Perth in a kilt, his testicles bared to the elements.'

The speech came the day after Mr Cameron had claimed in the House of Commons that the SNP were sending out hit squads of grey-shirted über-thugs in jackboots to intimidate business leaders who dared speak up against independence. When asked to provide verification of his remarks, Mr Cameron cited matters of national security, but said that the claims would be substantiated when the relevant documents were released in thirty years' time.

21 July 2014

Westminster Turns Sights On Saltire In New Attack

The UK government in Westminster appeared to turn up the heat in the Referendum campaign again this morning when it was revealed that moves are being made to introduce an international ban on the use of the Saltire in Scotland, in the event of a Yes vote in September.

While there has been some speculation about the future of the Union Jack should Scotland secede from the Union, insiders believe that the government has no intention of altering the British flag, regardless of the outcome. Consequently, they are loath to allow Scots use of the Saltire.

'Re-designing the Union Jack would cost billions,' said one Tory party source. 'There'd be the flags to replace, the paperwork and graphics to be amended, plus there'd be all that merchandise which would suddenly be worthless. Think of the work carried out by six year-old children in Indonesia making crappy Union Jack mugs and fridge magnets. Do we really want that hard toil to have been in vain? Good God, man, if nothing else, think of all the unsold Union Jack underpants.'

With the St Andrew's cross remaining an integral part of the Union flag, Westminster appears keen to be seen retaining ownership of the cross, and quite possibly of St Andrew himself. Insiders believe that David Cameron is drawing up secret plans to extend the use of the St Andrew's cross across a much broader spectrum than currently exists, building on the fact that the saltire is already one of the most widely-used designs in heraldry, flag-design and international symbology. The coming months will see the Bank of England issue a new £10 note bearing the image of St Andrew, St Andrew will be named the patron saint of the England football team, and there will be a new line of government-issue St Andrew's cross BDSM equipment, released through NS&I. Proposed advertising for the latter is believed to feature Theresa May and Michael Gove.

As soon as iScotland attempts to fly the flag as being representative of the nation, Westminster will pounce with an army of international lawyers and diplomats, intent on blocking them at every turn.

'Let there be no mistake,' Dr Ian Shackleton of the Glasgow School of Politics and Football told me this morning, as we spoke in his refurbished office on the 98th floor of the magnificent new Commonwealth Games Norovirus Complex in the city's east end, 'things are going to get ugly. Everything is on the table, not just the Saltire. You want to wear tartan on your wedding day? You want to eat porridge for breakfast? Good luck, my friend. If there's a Yes vote in September, Westminster lawyers will be ready, and they will bring the rain. If nothing else, iScotland will spend the first 50 years of its life in court fighting just to use its own name, fly its own flag, and deep fry its own burgers in a bun.'

Nicola Sturgeon was said to be outraged, although sources close to the Deputy First Minister privately admit that she's pretty much outraged about one thing or another on a daily basis. 'She had that nippy sweetie face on one day when the wind changed,' said one SNP insider who wished to remain anonymous.

The belief that Prime Minister Cameron will stop at nothing to prevent iScotland retaining any sort of national identity was confirmed later this morning, when it was reported that air traffic controllers for the entire British Isles have been instructed to prevent planes crossing each other's flight paths on sunny days, so that there will be no inadvertent Saltires created in the sky by white contrails against a clear blue background. The head of National Air Traffic Services UK refused to comment.

Despite their indignation at the Prime Minister's latest assault on Scottish identity, sources close to the First Minister, Alex Salmond, have indicated that designs for a new national flag are already being discussed, and that Holyrood is considering renting out space on the flag to a sponsor, after the fashion of football clubs and the front of their team strips. Bidders to be Scotland's first ever flag sponsor include Buckfast, Greggs, the Taj Mahal restaurant and Oor Wullie.

The SNP are also believed to be planning to introduce an away flag for Scotland to use overseas.

Other Referendum News From The Past Week

Wednesday 16 July

In what is being seen as a major boost for the No campaign ahead of September's Referendum on Scotland's future, the Westminster government today announced that six of the eight UK sites being considered for the first real-life Jurassic Park in the UK are in Scotland. The SNP dismissed the reports as a publicity stunt and stated that the only way to guarantee dinosaurs on the streets of Scotland was a vote for independence.

The UK is thought to be leading the way as scientists strive to recreate the dinosaur park of the successful movie franchise, and now Westminster is keen to let Scotland know that there is a 75 per cent chance that the site chosen for the park will be north of the border. The final decision will be announced on 19 September.

'It has been over 65 million years since dinosaurs were seen in Scotland,' said Prime Minister David Cameron, making the announcement, 'thanks to isolationist policies of successive independent Scottish monarchies and chancellorships throughout the centuries. Now, as part of Great Britain, the people of Scotland will once more have the opportunity to feed baby chickens to velociraptors.'

Mr Cameron claimed that lessons had been learned from the movies of the same name and that every precaution would be taken to ensure that there would be no breaches of security of the type that resulted in people getting eaten. 'Let me be absolutely clear about this,' he said. 'In the last twenty years, scientists have perfected the non-breeding gene that Richard Attenborough got so badly wrong. We'll also make sure that there are no big fat guys stealing stuff.'

Having brought Dolly the cloned sheep to the world, scientists in Scotland are now at the forefront of dino-replication. However, some paleontologists remain to be convinced about placing the park in Scotland.

'Dinosaurs and Scotsmen,' said Dr Alan Grant, of the Glasgow School of Diplodocus Studies, 'two species separated by 65 million years of evolution – give or take 64.9 million years – will just be suddenly thrown back into the mix together. How can we possibly have the slightest idea what to expect? Someone's going to get chibbed.'

The Prime Minister was at pains to point out that there would be a high percentage of female dinosaurs. The SNP, however, were unimpressed with the Prime Minister's announcement. 'They're just making shit up,' a source quoted a friend of a party insider saying. 'Next they'll say Scotland's going to get a space station.'

The sites shortlisted in Scotland for the dinosaur park include St Kilda, Ailsa Craig, Gruinard Island and Great Cumbrae.

28 July 2014

Darling Promises To Make Independence Sound Even More Apocalyptic

It was a subdued Alistair Darling who spoke to a smaller than usual media pool this morning. With journalists flocking to the Commonwealth Games to report sunshine, medals, success and an outpouring of exuberance, the audience for the High Commissioner of Better Together and his bleak tales of impending doom was reduced to little less than a handful. And although Darling's place in the BT pecking order has been the cause of speculation for some time, with most assuming his jacket to be on a peg shooglier than that of any on a wall in Gaza, the Chief Doomsayer Pursuivant of All Scotland is still taking every opportunity to grab a microphone and tell voters just how apocalyptically awful things are going to be in the event of a Yes vote.

'One need only look at the sad state of the world today,' said Mr Darling, preparing to invoke every bad thing that has happened on Planet Earth in the last few weeks to aid his argument, 'to see the precarious position in which Scotland will find itself. Look at Libya, the Central African Republic, Nigeria, Ukraine, Syria, Gaza, Somalia, Iraq,

Russian imperialism, Sino-Japanese tension, plane crashes every few days, the Ebola virus, South Sudan, Egypt, Afghanistan... Look at all the suffering, murder, death, horror and tragedy. That's what awaits an independent Scotland. The SNP think iScotland will be on the list of Scandinavian countries. But it won't. It will be on the list of shame, misery and fear. Think of how bad things could possibly get, and then multiply it by fifty.'

Later Mr Darling handed out plague masks which he advised people to start wearing within five minutes of confirmation of a Yes vote. In the event of a No vote, he requested that the masks be returned so they can be sold back to West Africa.

'The warnings, from both sides, are only going to get worse,' says political and footballing über-commentator, Dr Ian Shackleton. Speaking in his 98th floor office in the new William Wallace Freedom Centre at the heart of Glasgow's Revolution District, Dr Shackleton is pessimistic about the course of the debate over the coming weeks. 'Better Together are the ones with the well-deserved reputation for doom-merchantry, but don't think the Yes campaign are above it. As the weeks pass, more and more are we hearing baleful and threatening visions of the future of Scotland within the UK. Ironic, since they are so quick to accuse Better Together of negativity. Nevertheless, Alistair Darling remains the Prince of Peril.'

Analysts estimate that every time Alistair Darling opens his mouth, 4.7 people in Scotland attempt suicide.

This morning, warming to his theme, Mr Darling issued a list of seven key disasters that are likely to befall Scotland in the event of independence:

- There will be a race for businesses to head south of the border. Unemployment will hit record levels, and poverty will sweep across the nation.

- Impoverishment will breed ethnic division, and by the end of the year there will be over two million refugees. Unable to cross into rUK, they will be forced to walk into the sea, where they will lead aquatic lives in freezing temperatures off the coast of Fife.

- This year's long warm summer, following on from the mild, damp winter, will turn Scotland into a Lost World with giant insects and spiders. There will be entirely new forms of disease with which iScotland's neophyte health service will be unable to cope.

- Everyone will die and Scotland will become a theme park for giant rats.

- The stars will never be seen above Scotland again, as the air will be filled with choking smoke from the funeral pyres of five million dead.

- Scotland will become a ping pong ball in Cold War II leading to global destruction and the annihilation of the entire human race.

- Scotland will never win the Eurovision Song Contest.

In response to this staggeringly dramatic series of predictions, the SNP had nothing. Nicola Sturgeon spoke to the BBC, but had to break off the interview when she started crying. Alex Salmond, meanwhile, was said to have blubbed uncontrollably most of the morning, before finally being given a sedative and collapsing, exhausted, into his pizza chair.

Later in the afternoon Mr Darling was expected to accompany Death on a fact-finding trip to the Middle East.

Other Referendum News From The Past Week

Wednesday 23 July

Alex Salmond surprised the world this evening when he used his speech at the opening ceremony of the Commonwealth Games to declare war on England. Bare-chested and wearing a kilt stained with the blood of a thousand skewered English lords, the First Minister rallied the audience to avenge hundreds of years of English oppression. The dancers and singers of the Games opening ceremony were then revealed to be a crack team of ninja assassins, who quickly ethnically cleansed the arena of all true-born Englishmen, including Rod Stewart.

Hazel Irvine, commentating for the event on BBC television, was criticised by users of social media, for saying glibly, 'Well, no one saw that coming,' when the slaughter of the England team was over. Giant Tom wrote on Twitter: 'All respect lost 4 HI. Just Gabby for me from now on. Lol!!'

Although the First Minister had been warned by Scottish Secretary, Alistair Carmichael, not to politicise the Games, Mr Salmond's staff were thought to be working on several different drafts of his speech. It is understood that Mr Salmond – described as being light-headed and giddy after receiving a surprise kiss from John Barrowman – only decided at the last minute to issue the declaration of war, as he found himself in an independence sort of mood.

Although it is believed that the Games will proceed as planned, insiders reckon that the repercussions of the evening that some social media users are already calling 'That thing that was on the telly', will continue for some time.

'Let me be absolutely clear,' said Prime Minister David Cameron, 'something is going to happen as a result of this. Decisions will be taken. Sanctions will be made. There's nothing that won't come into play, just as soon as we have agreement with our European partners.'

Statisticians have calculated that Britain has never been in agreement with its European partners.

Speaking later, Mr Salmond played down the incident. Stating that he had merely welcomed everyone to the Games and invited them to participate in the true spirit of the Commonwealth, he added, 'If some chose to misrepresent my words and use them as cover for taking vengeance for a thousand years of Westminster subjugation, I can hardly be blamed.'

Some political analysts indicated that it was likely that Mr Salmond's words were misheard due to his mouth being crammed full of Tunnock's Tea Cakes.

4 August 2014

We Come To It At Last, The Great Political Debate Of Our Time

Frost/Nixon. Ali/Foreman. Murrow/McCarthy. Montgomery/Rommel. Disraeli/Gladstone. Now, to that pantheon of greatness, will be added Salmond/Darling.

The Commonwealth Games are over, the summer in Scotland has ground to a halt on the back of endless rains sweeping in from the polar north, the Referendum that the whole world has been talking about for the last two years is almost upon us, and now, before a worldwide television audience of over two billion, it gets serious.

All the bickering, all the negativity, all the preening and the absurdity, from the SNP's intention to introduce the Scottish Imperial Shekel to the sight of David Cameron and George Galloway embracing topless on the same platform, has led to this moment. The battle of giants. The clash of Titans. The meeting of intellectual and political behemoths. Professor X and Magneto. Goliath and Goliath.

'For sure,' said Dr Ian Shackleton, of the Glasgow School of Politics and Football, 'the SNP were unhappy that David Cameron refused to step up to the mike, but what was the PM supposed to do? The last living Conservative voter in Scotland died late last year. When a Scottish voter looks at David Cameron, they see the zombie love child of Dick Dastardly and Lizzie Borden.'

Looking across the golden spires of the city from his 98th floor office in the city's magnificent new Usain Bolt The Shit Tower, Shackleton reflected on the man who has been chosen to replace the Prime Minister in the most highly anticipated political debate since the time of the ancient city states of Greece.

'The Prime Minister may be gone, but in his place we have this man who's been a political hero to a generation,' said Shackleton. 'Sure, some people think Alistair Darling is the bad guy in an episode of Scooby Doo, before he takes his mask off. But show me a political heavyweight and I'll show you the contempt of the unworthy.'

Both First Minister Salmond, and Better Together übereyebrowspitzenreiter Darling are known to have been locked together with advisors for the last two weeks, twenty hours a day, practising. Tension in both camps is running high, with some reports indicating that Mr Salmond alone has worked his way through 17 practice opponents, many of whom are thought to have been psychologically crushed, with at least two likely to never speak again.

'These two men are coiled springs,' said Professor Malcolm Connery of the Glasgow Institute of Special Things. 'Every argument, every political point, every nuance of every topic is at their fingertips. This is going to be Borg/McEnroe times a thousand.'

Nevertheless, this great debate is about to be conducted in the shadow of the most tumultuous period in world affairs since the end of the Second World War, and political analysts, as well as friends of political analysts, foresee inherent troubles for the First Minister in the litany of horror in recent events.

For two years now Better Together have attempted to play on the uncertainty of independence. Now, almost as though it has been planned, the world suddenly seems like a much more uncertain place than it was at the start of the year. Every week that goes by seems to add a new outrage threatening to engulf us all, be it the spread of the Ebola virus, Cold War II leading to total Armageddon, or all Scottish teams being eliminated from Europe by the middle of August.

'Suddenly life seems terribly fragile,' says Dr Shackleton. 'Sure, independence might work. Things might be better, and maybe every single one of those arguments that the Yes campaign have been making are bang on. Maybe there really is the biggest oil field in the known universe off the coast of Millport. But if the Russians are just about to invade, or there's to be a super tsunami or we're all going to die of Ebola, it doesn't take much to see that the problems of Scotland's independence don't amount to a hill of beans in this crazy world.'

To counter the unforeseen drama of world events, Yes campaigners are thought to be pursuing a conspiracy theory agenda, suggesting that everything bad happening in the world today is as a result of Westminster manipulation.

'Wouldn't put anything past those bastards,' said a source close to an SNP spin doctor. 'Look at history, look at the Opium Wars, that was one of theirs. All this stuff that's filling the news, can you honestly say you don't detect the black hand of Westminster behind it all?'

Nevertheless, a friend of an unnamed source close to an SNP insider is known to have suggested that the party leadership were wrong to have been so insistent on the removal of Trident. With nuclear war shaping up to be slotted into the world's agenda some time in the next fourteen to eighteen months, people are beginning to ask if Scotland really wants to be left without a nuclear option.

'If everyone on the planet is going to be vaporised or burned horribly to death in screaming agony, Scotland can't just be on the sidelines,' said one Conservative Party insider. 'We have to retain the capacity to be at the heart of that kind of f***-witted stupidity.'

Much remains to be made clear, and tomorrow night, as the world watches in wonder at the pinnacle of political debate, all will be revealed. The pieces are falling into place. At last the bitter taste of the Lamont/Sturgeon debacle will be banished. Scotland stands on the precipice. History will be made. A king will be crowned.

Or maybe you just want to watch Rangers v Hibs on the BBC.

11 August 2014

Salmond Announces 'SNP For No' Movement As Balance Of Power Shifts

Seeking to protect his position as First Minister and leader of the SNP following last week's independence debate car crash, Alex Salmond used a photoshoot at a dairy farm in Perth this morning to unexpectedly launch a new SNP For No movement, as a counter to Labour For Yes.

Sensing the growth of opposition within his own party amid calls for him to be usurped by deputy Nicola Sturgeon, 44, Mr Salmond reportedly sat down with his personal policy advisors over the weekend and arrived at the new strategy, looking to appeal to SNP voters who are not yet ready for Scotland to become independent.

'Let me be absolutely clear about this,' said Mr Salmond, speaking to the press while milking a cow, 'I want Scotland to be independent, and one day Scotland will be independent. But, you know, I think everyone's getting a wee bitty carried away with this independence talk. It's all currency this, and sterling that, and aliens attacking from space the next thing. Let's everybody calm down and talk about this sensibly over a coffee and a doughnut.'

Accepting that he had been rushed into the independence vote ten years ahead of schedule, largely thanks to the rank incompetence of Scottish Labour which had handed the SNP the majority government in 2011, political insiders believe the First Minister intends to push for a No vote, then cull the party of his opponents and supporters of Ms Sturgeon, before taking a more measured approach to independence. It is believed he will aim for a decisive vote in 2024, by which time Mr Salmond will be 87.

'On the one hand, Alex Salmond makes Iain Gray and Johann Lamont look like Kyle Lafferty at a convention of Eusébios,' says Dr Ian Shackleton, of the Glasgow School of Politics and Football, 'but ultimately, he's thinking about his own legacy as much as any politician.'

Looking out over the majestic marble domes of Glasgow's south side in the weak August sunshine, Dr Shackleton continues in pensive mood. 'Some suspect that the First Minister intentionally torpedoed the debate last week. If Yes wins September's vote, it will be by the narrowest of margins. There will be resentment from England, there will be resentment from a large minority in Scotland. Things will be ugly, and he will be remembered as the politician who brought the ugly.'

Political analysts believe that the campaign was supposed to be about re-shaping the agenda, to get Scotland talking about independence, with a view to building a groundswell of opinion leading to a large majority vote in 2024. Now, however, thanks to the energy of grassroots Yes campaigners coupled with a Better Together campaign that has channelled Mr Bean and multiplied it by East Stirling, Salmond finds himself facing the possibility of a victory that was not supposed to happen for another decade.

'There's no question that was why he started banging on about aliens and driving on the wrong side of the road,' says Dr Shackleton. 'There's no doubt that was why he treated the Plan B question like it was contaminated with the Ebola virus. Mr Salmond has one of the finest political minds of his generation. In my opinion, he came across as Kermit the Frog because he wanted to come across as Kermit the Frog.'

A secret memo released to the impartial wing of the BBC has revealed the First Minister's seven-point plan, which tells us as much about his own political ambition as it does about his plans for the future of Scotland:

- engineer an heroic failure in next month's vote, of the kind familiar to Scots from many World Cup group stage eliminations
- purge the party of Sturgeon supporters, replacing them with his own loyal servants
- progress the Scottish independence debate,

building a consensus away from the glare and passion of an actual vote

- hold a new Referendum in 2024, which will pass with a predicted Yes vote of at least 75%
- become iScotland's first supreme Chancellor
- build a 200ft monument to himself to tower over Princes Street in Edinburgh
- invade England, creating a Greater Scotland, extending as far south as the Humber

'The debate has got away from Mr Salmond,' says Shackleton. 'It's similar to states sponsoring small terrorists groups, then suddenly, before they know it, the terrorist group has outgrown it and is knocking on the door of the kingdom threatening to blow it up. Salmond has lost control. The genie is out the bottle, and he's learning that while you can put the Pringles back in the can, you can't turn mince back into steak.'

Announcing his new SNP For No movement, Mr Salmond was in boisterous mood. 'Come with me on a journey,' he told a crowd of cheering farm animals. 'The pillars of western society are collapsing around us. Let us not add to the collapse by breeding strife at home. Let us sit back and wait, and when the UK has fallen so low that it's being propped up by loans from Niger, then we will make our move.'

Later Mr Salmond visited a cheese factory where he promised workers that cheese would remain a central part of Scotland's future.

18 August 2014

'Westminster Is Ours Too' Claims Salmond

In a surprise weekend development, First Minister and SNP leader*, Alex Salmond, announced that Scotland would seek to continue to use the Houses of Parliament in London in the event of a Yes vote.

(*as at time of writing)

'The Palace of Westminster belongs to Scotland too,' Mr Salmond told a crowd of cheering schoolchildren at a primary school in Strachur, 'and there's absolutely nothing anyone can do to stop us using it.'

It is not yet clear whether Mr Salmond intends that the Scottish parliament should sit in session in London, or whether plans are being made to move the Palace of Westminster to Scotland, brick by brick. While the No campaign refused to reveal cost figures for either plan, a Better Together insider suggested that both options would have significant financial implications.

'I doubt anyone is surprised by this move,' Dr Ian Shackleton of the Glasgow School of Politics and Football told me this morning, 'if you consider just how rank awful the building in Holyrood is. It was supposed to be cutting edge, sitting in the land, architecturally magnificent. Now it looks like that school project you made in Primary 6. At the time you thought it was awesome, then you take it out the cupboard fifteen years later, and you're like, oh dear, that's really crap, no wonder Mrs Hamilton told me never to try to make anything ever again.'

From the outset it has been clear that the SNP strategy was to keep as much continuity from the UK as possible, to try to attract voters naturally conservative in nature. From the Pound to the Queen and the BBC, the First Minister's approach has almost been one of Independence Lite, to the dismay of more radical nationalists. Now, in the face of a Better Together campaign that has insisted iScotland won't get the Pound, they can only have the Royals that no one else wants, like Camilla and Eugenie, and that they can have BBC3 and that's it, Mr Salmond is intent on raising the stakes.

As well as continued use of the Houses of Parliament, Mr Salmond indicated that an independent Scotland would be pushing for:

- ownership of one-tenth of Buckfast Abbey
- one in ten episodes of Downton Abbey to be made in the Highlands
- that one-tenth of Crossrail should run through Dundee
- half of one of the surviving members of the Monty Python team to be declared Scottish

- one-tenth of MI6 should be relocated to Edinburgh and known as MI6/10ths

'We currently have just under one tenth of the population of the UK,' said Mr Salmond. 'Accordingly, having rounded that number up to make it easier, it is in no way unjust that we should be entitled to one tenth of the assets of the UK, and to continue to use those assets as we see fit.'

A Better Together spokesperson responded, that by using the same argument, the UK was entitled to nine-tenths of all previously government funded projects in Scotland, and that the decent parts of the A9 would be removed for use on the A66.

'It's all subtext,' said Shackleton, as we spoke in his 98th floor office in the all-new Midge Ure Memorial Tower overlooking Glasgow's Band Aid District. 'No one seriously supposes that the Scottish government is going to meet in London. No one really thinks that London is going to take nine-tenths of the Garrison in Millport. What it points to, however, is how acrimonious this is going to get if there's a Yes vote. Everything is on the table, and this isn't going to be some cosy negotiation, with a bunch of old duffers sitting agreeably in a club, drawing straight lines on a map, and spending more time debating which port to have after dinner. It's going to be like Stalingrad multiplied by The Towering Inferno.'

Earlier Mr Salmond attempted to take the heat out the debate over the Pound, by confirming that his government are in negotiations with the embattled land of Mordor with a view to forging a currency union. While Mordor originally held sway over men, elves and dwarves, in recent times their influence has diminished significantly. Some economists believe that a fiscal union with an independent Scotland would be a bold starting point for Mordor, as it begins to attempt to claw its way back into a position of power.

While some pundits question the motives of the SNP leader, others are quick to point out that the path from the Bank of England to the Bank of Mordor is a short one. Nevertheless, most commentators urge caution, albeit not always for the reasons that one might think.

'Mr Salmond is going to look mighty foolish, walking out on David Cameron into a pact with Sauron, if it turns out that Cameron and Sauron are, as many suspect, one and the same person,' says Professor Malcolm Connery, of the Glasgow Institute of Special Things. 'The similarities between Cameron and Sauron are well documented. Neither of them needs to be leader, they just choose to do it out of badness, they're both happy for their people to live in austerity, and from a distance they both look like a pussy.'

At this stage it is still too early to say what citizens of an independent Scotland might be using for currency come March 2016 – chickens, blocks of cold porridge out the kitchen drawer, and the new Scottish Imperial Shekel remain favourite – which can be said for much of the picture surrounding iScotland. Better Together have attempted to paint an image of total bewilderment, something in which political pundits reckon they are finally beginning to succeed.

Meanwhile, the weekend opinion polls were the usual mixed bag depending, as ever, on who commissioned the poll in the first place. The result was that the poll of polls showed, for the first time, Don't Knows moving into the lead with 37%, ahead of No 34% and Yes 29%. If Don't Knows win the vote on 18 September, analysts believe Scotland will be set to live in a state of total confusion for the next three hundred years.

25 August 2014

Secret Downing Street Memo Reveals Shock and Awe Plan

With some polls indicating the Referendum race becoming too close to call, the leaking of a secret Downing Street memo has revealed that not only is Prime Minister David Cameron contemplating the possibility of defeat, but that his aides are suggesting a raft of shock and awe tactics within 24 hours of a Yes vote.

The memo, written by an unnamed senior civil servant, advises Mr Cameron that a Yes vote would be incredibly damaging not only to him personally, but to the chances of the Conservative Party being re-elected in May 2015. The memo lists a tranche of dramatic measures that Westminster should immediately implement following the vote, to seize the news cycle, restore the Prime Minister's credibility and instantaneously prick the bubble of SNP celebration.

'If the voters of Scotland want independence, then let's not make them wait. They can have it, starting at 9am on 19 September 2014,' the memo begins. It then lists more than twenty dramatic interventions the government should make, including:

- setting up controls on all cross-border roads
- building a fence the length of the border
- suspending or blocking all flights to and from Scotland
- closing down all UK government offices in Scotland
- stopping all funding to Holyrood
- redeploying all troops south of the border
- use UK influence and veto to block Scotland's membership of all international organisations including, but not limited to, the UN, WHO, EU, NATO, FIFA, UEFA and the Eurovision Song Contest
- remove as much hard currency as possible from Scotland, meaning that supplies of the Pound would quickly dwindle, forcing the hurried introduction of the Scottish Imperial Shekel or a barter system
- take every action open to them to crush the Scottish economy

Political analysts, such as Dr Ian Shackleton of the Glasgow School of Politics and Football, are in no doubt that plans to immediately eject Scotland from the Union are being seriously considered.

'This isn't about Project Fear or scaremongering,' he told me this morning, as we talked in his 98th floor office in the new Lulu Grande Tower at the heart of Glasgow's bucolic north side. 'The leaking of this memo was not supposed to happen. These ideas are a genuine consideration, stemming from genuine resentment and bitterness. Imagine how England is going to feel the day after a Yes vote. They're going to have been dumped, and it's happened on Cameron's watch. Hundreds of years from now the likes of Blair and Brown and Major will have long been forgotten, but the name Cameron will be remembered forever as the man who lost the Union. Only by acting quickly will he be able to save his premiership from becoming the biggest dead duck of the last 300 years.'

If the plans work out as Westminster intends, Scotland would be bankrupt from day one, with government offices closing down, and banks moving south of the border. Rather than the following morning's newspapers being filled with photos of cheering crowds and a beaming Alex Salmond, they would have pictures of long queues for bread, garages with no petrol, starving hospitals and boarded up children.

'And let's not suppose the world would stop it happening,' continued Shackleton. 'The world either wouldn't care, or would be unable to act. The Yes campaign is often seen as one of breaking away from the old establishment. But the British establishment still has a large say in the running of Everything. Yes voters may find that there's literally no escape. Westminster is basically aiming to say, you can be part of the UK, or you can be North Korea. Scottish voters might think they're sticking the middle finger up at Westminster, but they're going to find that Westminster's middle finger reaches places you don't even want to think about.'

There are also believed to be two other memos circulating in Downing Street outlining potential future Westminster approaches towards an independent Scotland. One suggests that the UK sets up a committee to work with Scotland to ease towards a smooth transition, accommodating Scotland as much as possible while still protecting the interests of the remaining nations. In Downing Street circles, this has become mockingly known as 'The Rapture Scenario', because it's never going to happen.

The other memo suggests that Westminster should openly congratulate Scotland and look to work with it across all sectors, while secretly briefing, planning and fighting against it behind the scenes, hoping to delay long past 24 March 2016, the date planned by the SNP for Scottish independence.

'This perhaps is the most likely option,' said Shackleton, 'although it does Cameron little good in the short term. They would postpone all discussions until after the Westminster elections next May, then they would couple idle promises with obfuscation to try to delay independence until after the next Holyrood election. Moves would be made to replace Johann Lamont as leader of Scottish Labour with someone capable of energising the innate Scottish socialist vote – albeit no one actually knows who that is – so that suddenly you had an anti-independence government in Holyrood.'

'What would happen then?' I asked Dr Shackleton, as we stood at his office window, looking out at the plumes of smoke coming from the east, where Russian troops were clashing with the Islamic State as they fought for control in the forests around Airdrie.

'No one knows,' he said. 'It's going to be like the Alamo multiplied by Black Swan.'

While no one yet knows which path Westminster will choose to follow in the event of a Yes vote, pictures have begun to appear on the Internet, even this morning, of fencing materials being stockpiled in the north of England, amid suggestions that all English people living in Scotland are being advised to cast their vote on 18 September and then immediately head south of the border, in case of reprisals.

As fears grow that the separation between iScotland and rUK could be nastier and more contentious than many have up until now suspected, a number of celebrities posted comments on Twitter, as if that would make any difference.

Rubeus Hagrid, Keeper of the Keys at Hogwarts School of Witchcraft and Misery, wrote, 'There's a shitstorm coming, Harry.'

1 September 2014

'Game of Chess Without Pieces' Nears Endgame

The world stands at the precipice: war rages in Ukraine, as Europe looks on in majestic impotence, unable to fathom a confrontation that threatens to consume the continent; the Middle East collapses beneath a cataclysm of horror, the Islamic State closing up the walls of their caliphate with the severed heads of non-believers, while Syria burns, Israel and Palestine limp angrily from ceasefire to ceasefire, and Shia and Sunni head inexorably towards a final conflict across the region; India and Pakistan square up in Kashmir, entering a state of near-war, as protestors descend on the government in Islamabad; the Taleban prepare to re-conquer Afghanistan; China belligerently extends its influence over the South China Sea; the world barely notices as ethnic cleansing continues in CAR and the world's newest independent state, South Sudan, is buried beneath the weight of war, slaughter and mass forced migration; the Ebola virus runs riot in West Africa, decimating countries too poor and war-ravaged to be able to fight an invisible enemy; Libya disintegrates into a Somalia-esque stateless hell; the leader of the Western world stands helplessly in a tan suit, wishing away the next two and a half years; a time for great men and women, a time for a great leader to emerge from the morass, sees nothing but despots and incompetents; and someone threw an egg at Jim Murphy.

'It's all kicking off,' says Dr Ian Shackleton, of the Glasgow School of Politics and Football. Speaking to me this morning from his office on the 98th floor of the epic new Johann Lamont Memorial Tower in the city's Out-Of-Its-Depth District, Shackleton flicked through the news channels as he talked. 'It was interesting when asked the other night if the Referendum debate was getting ill-tempered, Darling said yes, and Salmond, of course, said that it wasn't. But are we at this stage yet?' he asks, indicating the television, which is showing Russian troops pouring over the border into Ukraine dressed as random pieces of shrubbery. 'Probably not. What we have at the moment is more of a game of chess. Without the pieces. Or the strategy. Or the grandmasters. Or the wit, the intelligence or the strategic vision. So, actually, not so much like a game of chess. It's more of a naked mud wrestling contest with clothes and no mud.'

While many political analysts disagree on what kind of sporting metaphor best suits the Referendum debate, they all agree on where the momentum lies. The Yes campaign is on the charge, while the No campaign is throwing the occasional sand bag into the middle of the tsunami.

'They don't know what to do,' says Shackleton. 'It's almost as if it hasn't occurred to them to suggest that there's anything good about Britain. Like they're embarrassed to say anything nice about it. The Yes campaign have been traducing Britain and its parliament since the debate started, as if the country is Syria multiplied by an Adam Sandler film. What have the No campaign had in reply? The Lady With A Mug Of Tea, in an advert that was the Armageddon of toe-curling embarrassment.'

After a car crash of a week left the two sides more or less neck and neck in the polls, voters are awaiting Better Together's next move with a sense of nervous anticipation.

'Sadly, it's like waiting for the next episode of Mr Bean, rather than the next speech from Nelson Mandela,' says Shackleton. 'And everybody hates Mr Bean.'

In an attempt to turn things around, Better Together are believed to be working on:

- a written British constitution enshrining Scotland as 'a place of significant interest'
- a new advert in which the Lady With A Mug Of Tea gets brutally murdered by a gang of Yes-supporting zombies
- celebrity *It's A Knockout*, with teams led by Douglas Alexander, Ruth Davidson, Charles Kennedy and Princess Anne, presented by Stuart Hall from his prison cell
- a two-week stump speech tour from Gordon Brown, accompanied by celebrity chefs to

transform all the food thrown at him into delicious
fresh meals to be handed out at food banks

- Prime Minister Cameron, wearing a ginger wig, in
a full-frontal naked *Cosmopolitan* centrefold

Whichever move they choose, and analysts have little
doubt that it'll be the wrong one, at least voters know that
we are finally nearing the end.

'Of course,' says Dr Shackleton, as he stares out at the
mile-high plumes of smoke coming from the burning
forests of the Trossachs, 'the end of the campaign, good
or bad, will just be the start of something else. All we can
do is hope for the best, and that the worst is nothing more
than another game of really crap chess.'

Other Referendum News From The Past Week

Wednesday 27 August

Alistair Darling has promised to visit Pyongyang 'as soon
as possible' to personally receive the coveted Kim Jong-il
Gold Medal For Services In Ruining Political Debate. The
award, made at the discretion of the government of the
Democratic People's Republic of Korea, is given on an ad
hoc basis, but the committee in Pyongyang had no
hesitation in awarding Mr Darling the prize following
Monday evening's Fright Night At The Museum.

The statement from the committee begins:

'History teaches us the dangers of political discourse. The People must learn that their leaders are always right and that discussion and debate are to the detriment of society. Alistair Darling, with a performance of such staggering and apocalyptic incompetence, showed the workers that debate is useless. His performance was like 9/11 times 2,356. If every political debate was this bad, it would soon die out.'

Dr Shackleton, like other political analysts, is unsurprised by the award.

'Yes, Alex Salmond was bad, so bad in fact that you might say that he also lost the debate. He just didn't lose it as much as Darling, who came third out of two. Darling, of course, created the problem for himself by marginally raising the bar after the first debate, but by God, on Monday evening he didn't just lower the bar again, he burned the bar, cluster bombed it, stuck it up his backside and then shat it out straight into a plague-riddled septic tank.'

Praising Mr Darling's finger-pointing, stammering, repetition and eyebrows, the Committee particularly noted the expert way in which, over the previous two weeks he had forced the Yes campaign into a corner over currency, had more or less drawn from them that Plan B would be Sterlingisation, and then, rather than using carefully constructed economic reason to argue against Sterlingisation, he continued to say 'but what's Plan B?' even though by this point there were single cell amoeba that knew what Plan B was.

'It was a masterclass,' the statement concludes. 'We hope Mr Darling visits Pyongyang as quickly as possible, where he will be given the appropriate haircut.'

Later, having been told what the award was for, Mr Darling repeatedly asked what the award was for.

8 September 2014

Anglo-Scottish Border Likely To Be Re-Drawn In Event Of Yes Vote

As the polls tighten ever further, and London begins to see Scotland slip from its muculent grasp, all players in the Referendum debate are beginning to face up to the realities and possibilities of a Yes vote. While currency, Trident, the NHS and oil reserves have taken centre stage, political analysts predict that, as with any dispute between neighbouring nations, the argument over the border will come to outweigh all others.

This morning secret government memos, from both Westminster and Holyrood, have revealed that angry discussions have already taken place between the two powers on the subject. The current ninety-six mile border, running from the River Tweed in the east to the Solway Firth in the west, is considered by many to be unworkably ragged.

'The current wibbly-wobbliness of the border is totally unviable, will lead to disagreements within communities, and will make it prohibitively expensive to build the wall when it becomes required,' states one Westminster memo, written by an advisor to the Prime Minister. 'And there's no doubt that a wall will be required, sooner or later.'

Diplomats from both sides are in agreement that a straight line should be drawn across the country, on a latitudinal parallel.

'The drawing of straight lines on maps has worked well in so many different regions of the world,' says Dr Ian Shackleton, of the Glasgow School of Politics and Football. 'It's no surprise they want to do it here. America-Canada, that's worked out all right. There are some great borders in Africa that have served the continent well for over a hundred years. Perhaps there are still some teething problems with the Middle East, but I think we've learned the appropriate lessons.'

Naturally, however, there is disagreement about where the line should be drawn.

Political insiders and friends of political insiders believe that London want to see a straight line drawn directly across the map from Berwick-upon-Tweed – to be known as the 55.77th parallel – which would make places such as East Kilbride and Wishaw border towns, and everything south of there in England.

'No one doubts,' said an unnamed source in the Conservative Party, 'that the Borders in Scotland will vote to remain part of the Union. Fine, if the rest of Scotland wants to go independent, on you go. Be the South Sudan of the north, see if we care. But we're keeping the Borders, and we'll fight to extend the definition of that area as far north as possible. The 55.77th parallel might not roll off the tongue, but when it comes to the negotiations, it's going to be part of it, just as much as Trident, currency and who Andy Murray plays for at the next Olympics.'

Insiders believe that London will open negotiations by insisting that the border should be defined by the Antonine Wall, which ran north of Glasgow, from the Clyde to the Forth, and would therefore place both Edinburgh and Glasgow in England. One SNP insider described how, when first told of these demands, Alex Salmond 'exploded out of his pants.'

Meanwhile officials in Holyrood are determined that, at the very least Berwick-upon-Tweed should be included in Scotland, as it has been so often in the past, with some insiders stating that they will aim to have the border as far south as Derby. They would then be able to include powerhouse football teams such as Manchester City, Liverpool and Hull in the Scottish Premier League, as well as struggling smaller clubs such as Manchester United. Officials acknowledge that the downside of this plan is that it would, for the first time, give Scotland a land border with Wales.

Few, however, doubt that there won't be a great deal of upheaval.

'Rarely,' says Shackleton, as we speak in his office on the 98th floor of the new Ed Miliband Memorial Tower in the heart of the city's Cheese District, 'do arguments over land borders get resolved without one side drinking the blood of their enemies. Still, perhaps this one will be settled amicably over a spot of curling.'

In the likelihood that drawing straight lines on a map becomes contentious, it is believed that the zombified corpses of both Sir Mark Sykes and François Georges-Picot will be brought onto the negotiating teams as consultants.

Other Referendum News From The Past Week

Friday 5 September

With the Referendum momentum all going one way, and Better Together in desperate need of a bold plan to present to voters to combat the optimism and positivity of Yes Scotland, Prime Minister David Cameron yesterday promised sweeping changes in the way the United Kingdom will be governed in future.

Speaking to a cheering group of foreign exchange students at Stirling University on the first day of their Beginner's English course, Mr Cameron outlined his five-point plan for the future of Britain:

- the House of Lords would be abolished, and all members culled
- all powers, bar defence, diplomacy, the central bank and Eurovision Song Contest song selection would be placed in the hands of the parliaments of Scotland, England, Wales and Northern Ireland
- Westminster would become the seat of the English parliament
- a new streamlined, central, federal seat of UK government would be created, and situated in the grounds of the Garrison in Millport
- free Tunnock's Tea Cakes for everyone

'This,' says Dr Shackleton, 'is what the No campaign have been waiting for. A vision for the future. A bold statement of change in the UK.

'While there's an unmistakeable whiff of the Ally McLeod about the Yes campaign, you can't argue that it's captured the imagination of voters. Better Together thought they could rely on a message of It's Not Completely Shit, So Why Change Anything? and they've been found wanting. They didn't want any big ideas, because they like things the way they are.

'Now, however, they're faced with losing oil revenue, they're looking at a long and bitter border war, and then there's the likelihood of other world leaders mocking them openly on Twitter. They've had to face up to the need to think strategically about Britain's future. And while some commentators amongst the liberal elite might think it ethically questionable to kill all the members of the House of Lords, most agree that it would be, at least, electorally popular.'

Challenged on the costs of setting up the new parliament, Mr Cameron claimed that money saved from Lords' expenses, coupled with converting the Lords Chamber in the Palace of Westminster into a bingo hall complete with on-site Starbucks, Pizza Express and Hello Kitty! Tattoo Parlour would pay for the new Federal Millport Parliament Building four times over.

'Let me be absolutely clear about this,' said Mr Cameron, 'the UK national debt, which currently stands at £1.45trillion, will not increase by one penny because of this new plan.'

Commentators noted that by the time the Prime Minister had finished speaking, some two minutes later, the UK national debt had already increased to £1.53 trillion.

15 September 2014

Scotland To Be Independent 'By Christmas'

History will relate that there was little the No campaign did not try (bar common sense, optimism and presenting a vision.) Fear and bullying; negativity magnified by misanthropy; Big Gordon Brown making the worst comeback tour since the zombified corpse of Michael Jackson failed to sell out Blackpool Pier; promises and threats thrown around like a co-dependent lover; the Prime Minister blubbing like a small child while insisting that he's as Scottish as Rod Stewart; all this, and Ed Miliband stroking a dead cat and promising Scotland that he's going to be very upset if they vote Yes. Very upset indeed.

And yet, it comes to this. The polls are only going one way, the silent majority that the No campaign have talked about for so long have disappeared into the lost borderlands where Rory Stewart walks alone, and suddenly it looks like Better Together, through incompetence, ignorance and stupidity, will manage what the Nazis failed to do.

It is believed that David Cameron spent last night sitting in a bunker beneath Downing Street considering his options. As advisors came and went, some talked of Cameron losing his temper and shouting uncontrollably.

'He's lost the plot,' said one insider. 'He refuses to believe the No campaign has ground to a halt and is being driven back on every front.'

The Prime Minister is understood to be considering several options, including:

- screaming loudly while slamming his fist onto a map
- offering Alex Salmond half of Berkshire
- giving Scotland to Russia in return for peace on the Eastern Front
- feeding the CIA intelligence that Islamic terrorists have taken control of Edinburgh, then sitting back and watching the ensuing bunfight on CNN
- resigning, and hitting the brothels of Thailand for three self-destructive months of alcohol and cheap sex

On a grey Monday morning in Glasgow, I stand in the 98th floor office of political analyst Dr Ian Shackleton of the Glasgow School of Politics and Football in the magnificent new Jim Sillars Memorial Tower in the heart of the city's Revenge District. There is a stillness abroad, all the more noticeable following the riotous and colourful weekend of campaigning that engulfed the city.

The mood seems subdued, not just in this room, towering over the great conurbation, with a view out over the flat lands of Renfrewshire to the Western Isles and Bermuda in the far distance, but across the whole of the country. Independence is coming and many are wondering: will the great unstoppable wave of freedom be a flood of opium to a wounded soldier, or will it be a plague of the undead, leaving death, despair and the rotting corpse of false optimism in its wake?

'There's change afoot,' says Dr Shackleton, breaking a long silence. 'But people don't like change, not really. They talk about it, they dream about it, but when it comes to it, when the norm is threatened, they don't really like it. But it's happening now, and there's nothing they can do to stop it.'

'What about all those people marching on the BBC armed with torches and pitchforks?' I ask. 'They seem to want change.'

Shackleton seems vaguely curious, as if he hadn't realised that the city is besieged by mobs of angry villagers, looking to chase Nick Robinson back down the M74.

'If there's a Yes vote on Thursday, the Union will unravel quickly,' he says, warming to his theme. 'Some say that March 2016 is optimistic in timescale. In reality, Scotland will be independent before Christmas. The markets won't wait. No one will wait. The entire edifice of the United Kingdom will start to collapse, and it will only be saved by Scotland withdrawing immediately.'

There has been much talk in recent days of Capital Flight, although it was later revealed to have been a story about a new budget airline flying between Vienna, Edinburgh, Oslo and Madrid. Nevertheless, there's a nervousness in the air that you can taste.

'The No campaign misjudged the Scottish people,' says Shackleton. 'Westminster, these politicians, they believe everyone thinks like them. That's why they get so much wrong. That's why they've screwed up the Middle East, that's why they'll end up at war with Russia. And I don't know whose mind it is you change by employing pompous twattery, but it's certainly not the Scots.'

There has been much discussion about whether a close vote, either way, would lead to war, ethnic cleansing and terror. Dr Shackleton, however, thinks it's far more likely to lead to an outbreak of lawyers.

A recent FoI request revealed that both the Holyrood and Westminster governments had a full scrotum of lawyers going over every aspect of the other's campaign, in the hope of finding abuses of electoral law to use in litigation to annul the result. Jim Sillars's threat to 'annihilate with extreme prejudice every f***** that votes No' is just the kind of thing that will play into the lawyers' hands.

'The lawyers are coming,' says Shackleton. 'If there's a Yes vote, Friday will be a day of celebration, and Saturday will be the day that papers are filed to rescind the result.'

And then?

'And then Salmond acts quickly, spouting his well-rehearsed shtick about the sovereign will of the Scottish people, and declares independence. Whatever happens, it's going to be ugly.'

Political commentators, analysts, sources and crazy people on the Internet, are convinced that Thursday, regardless of the result, will only be the beginning.

'Even if there's a No vote,' says Shackleton, 'the walls have come crumbling down. It's the old planning application analogy. If you want to fight a housing development, No keep having to win over and over again. The guys who want to build the houses only have to win once. So maybe it won't be Alex Salmond and Nicola Sturgeon who win Scotland's independence, but it will be their bastard child, multiplied by Mel Gibson.'

I ask Dr Shackleton if he has any advice for those people yet to make up their minds. He turns to the other side of his office, and stares off into the grey distance, where the pounding of Russian heavy artillery meets the mournful ululation of the gulls over the Mount Vernon landfill site.

'Follow your stomach,' he says. 'Deep fry your vote and eat it with chips.'

Shortly afterwards I leave his office and walk slowly down ninety-eight flights of stairs out into the grim Glaswegian morning, stuck forever in the historic present.

22 September 2014

And In The End...

And in the end, it was the silent majority who spoke.

Those hundreds of thousands who cared not for two years of campaigning, who ignored every debate – from the Great Sturgeon/Lamont Disaster, to the Salmond/Darling *My Cock Is Bigger Than Your Cock* Double Header – who had never heard of the Scottish Imperial Shekel and who never knew that Vote No Borders was conceived in a PR office in Manhattan, the hundreds of thousands who just plain never wanted the Referendum to happen in the first place.

Perhaps, two years ago, they'd have thought that they probably wouldn't even bother voting. But in the end, when it seemed that the Union was in doubt, when the collapse of the United Kingdom seemed as certain as the fall of Gondor to the massed ranks of the Dark Lord, the silent majority appeared, like King Theoden and his men on the hill above the great plain, and rode to the rescue.

Was it all a fantasy? All the polls and the hype and the talk of how close it could be, was it all a myth created by Alex Salmond and the media in search of a good story?

This morning I spoke to renowned political analyst, Dr Ian Shackleton, of the Glasgow School of Politics and

Football. Standing in his office on the 98th floor of the recently completed Gordon Brown Memorial Tower at the heart of the city's Resurrection District, looking out over a vast landscape of burning SNP supporters, I find the doctor in grim mood.

'The nation is divided,' he tells me. 'Brother against sister, husband against wife, multi-millionaire against hardworking, poverty-stricken accountancy consultant. Westminster is stuck with this shambolic promise of more powers, and for the most part, the people who voted No would have voted No anyway. They don't care about more powers. Yes voters are left howling with rage, while Westminster mocks them and drinks the blood of Scottish benefit claimants. It won't end well.'

I remind Dr Shackleton that just over a week ago he predicted that Scotland would be independent by Christmas. He waves away the prediction with his usual avuncular charm.

'I was just making that shit up,' he says. 'In that,' he points out, 'I was not alone.'

Shackleton then outlines the six-point path he believes will lead to Scotland being independent by Christmas one year or another.

- having allowed his desperation to write cheques his political ability couldn't cash, Cameron is forced to renege on all his promises and no further powers are devolved

- Nicola Sturgeon puts on her Wonder Woman costume and her wee nippy sweetie face, hides her delight that the powers were not devolved, and uses it to crush the opposition at the next Holyrood election
- the SNP bide their time, wait for the UK overall to vote to leave the EU on the instructions of the right wing press, while Scotland votes overwhelmingly to stay, and then call another Referendum
- a distracted Westminster once more blunders into the vote, allowing the question to be posed as: *Should Scotland become independent from the murdering, rapacious, deceitful scum bastards in Westminster, allowing themselves to breathe the clean, fresh air of freedom, with free doughnuts?*
- a more focused SNP, having learned their lessons from the last time over the economy and currency, swoop like an unfettered eagle on the baby lamb of secession
- Scotland votes overwhelmingly for independence, and the campaign of 2014 becomes a path along the way, rather than a bloody footnote in history.

'It's coming,' says Shackleton. 'Inexorably, predictably, undeniably. It might be because of another vote, it might be because America tells the UK to split up and Westminster rolls over like an obedient servant, it might be because the United Kingdom finally collapses beneath the weight of Nigel Farage's arsehole. But it's coming.'

Political infighting quickly broke out following the No vote this weekend, with each of the three Westminster leaders putting as much distance between each other as they could, which was tricky, given that they all believe in the same capitalist, elitist system, that crushes workers and washes the pavements of Westminster with the tears of starving children.

Prime Minister David Cameron was said to have told Alex Salmond: 'Extra powers? I don't know no stinking extra powers.' Nick Clegg stated that he was absolutely determined to 'do the thing', although he couldn't remember what the thing was.

Ed Miliband, in temporary charge of the Labour party, failed to correctly pick out Scotland on the map, as a result of which he committed a future Labour government to an independent Suffolk.

'If they'd just played a decent game in the first place,' says Shackleton, 'they wouldn't have been panicked into this absurd pledge. Now they look like stupid multiplied by desperate and duplicitous. I doubt anyone would be surprised if this whole shambles doesn't end up with Sturgeon crushing Cameron's testicles in a vice fashioned from the last piece of shipbuilding equipment in Govan.'

Later a spokesperson for the Prime Minister denied that Mr Cameron had any balls in the first place.

'The government in Westminster need to hand over enough powers to make sure that Gordon Brown, Alistair

Darling and Scottish Labour in general aren't humiliated. At least, any more than they are by being Scottish Labour in the first place. That way the SNP won't get their majority government in Holyrood and there won't be another vote.'

Shackleton strokes his contemplative beard as he looks out east, over by the great plains around Shotts, where Russian troops are in hand-to-hand combat with an elite Libyan extremist militia. 'You humiliate Gordon Brown at your peril,' he says.

'Look at Obama since that time he only allowed Brown to meet him in the hotel kitchen. Hasn't been the same since. Obama can't buy a piece of legislation, all because he pissed off Big Gordon.'

The world is in flux. War with Russia looms, and we can only hope that it is Cold War 2, rather than World War 3 or Die Hard 6.

The Ebola virus threatens to burst the porous defences of West Africa and unleash the worldwide zombie apocalypse. The descent of the Middle East into a vast, never ending war zone continues to accelerate.

Manchester United are battling relegation and Celtic are five points off the top of the league.

For a brief moment, however, Scotland provided some certainty.

Nothing, however, lasts forever. The game is far from over, and now some say, just as in the final few days of the great Scottish Independence Referendum campaign of 2014, the very future of Scotland lies in the hands of Gordon Brown, the big man from Raith.

'Perhaps he can hold the Three Amigos' feet to the fire until their rocks melt in the sun,' remarks Dr Shackleton, 'or perhaps he will choose to depart with the remains of the half-time oranges, leaving the field to others.'

'Eternity,' adds the Doctor with a heavy sigh, pointing east to the oncoming collapse of western civilisation, 'waits for no man.'

Afterword

It is late November, and a weak autumn sun shines on Glasgow. Once again I find myself in the office of Dr Ian Shackleton, two and a half months since the end of the campaign. Or, more accurately, since the Referendum, as the campaign continues to this day, and will for years to come.

The weeks since the vote have been remarkable. The SNP, nominally on the losing side, have partied like winners, attracting new members by the trainload, while Nicola Sturgeon has played a sell-out series of gigs, performing songs such as 'Make You Feel My Love' and 'My Heart Will Go On' to packed audiences of screaming fans up and down the country. Meanwhile, Scottish Labour has been busy unloading double barrels of stupidity, in-fighting and bitterness into its own feet, amid a series of resignations, retirements and tactical retreats.

'These are dark times for the United Kingdom,' says Dr Shackleton, looking out the window of his 98th floor office of the recently completed Keir Hardie Memorial Tower in the city's Turning In His Grave District. 'English voters are fed up with traditional politics, so they turn to a party of ex-Conservative, white, middle-aged bankers, as though that'll change the system, while the utterly spineless Cameron and Miliband are too pusillanimous to do anything other than pander and fawn. And in this febrile political atmosphere, the SNP flourish using nothing but common sense and careful planning. Planning, one should add, that factored in losing the Referendum. These people know what they're doing, playing the long game. Scottish Labour look like they don't know which foot the left shoe fits on.'

The future of Scotland will not be decided in the coming weeks or even months, but once the shape of the next Westminster and Holyrood parliaments are known, it could well be that Scotland is looking down the barrel of Referendum II.

'Independence is coming,' says Shackleton, as we look east, from where darkness is quickly approaching. 'I'm sure of it, I can feel it in my water. But then, so is World War III and the end of civilisation as we know it here in the West of Scotland, so you might want to hold off on the celebratory bottle of Buckie until you see how that plays out.'

Some other books published by **LUATH** PRESS

100 Days of Hope and Fear

David Torrance
ISBN 978-1-910021-31-6 PBK
£9.99

Reading this diary back during the editing process it was clear that, like (Nate) Silver (the US polling guru whose view was that the Yes campaign had virtually no chance of victory), I got a lot of things wrong (including the likely margin of victory) but also many things broadly correct. At least I can plead, as journalists often do, that I was probably right at the time.

What can the people of Scotland – and other aspirant nations – learn from this seismic democratic event? Scotland's independence referendum on 18 September 2014 was the most significant ballot in Scotland's history. The 100 days up to 18 September was the official campaign period and the world's media was watching. David Torrance was there throughout, in front of the cameras, on the radio, in the newspapers, at the debates and gatherings, privy to some of the behind-the-scenes manoeuvrings.

100 Weeks of Scotland: A Portrait of a Nation on the Verge

Alan McCredie
ISBN 978-1-910021-60-6 PBK
£9.99

100 Weeks of Scotland is a revealing journey into the heart and soul of Scotland in the 100 weeks that led up to the independence referendum in September 2014.

From the signing of the Edinburgh Agreement through to the referendum and its immediate aftermath, this book charts a country in the grip of political debate. *100 Weeks of Scotland* is not simply a political book. It brings together stunning photography and stimulating commentary to capture a country in transition.

It examines Scotland in all its forms from its stunning landscapes to its urban sprawl to, most notably of all, its people as they live their lives in the run up to the most significant democratic event in their country's history. It is a portrait of a nation on the verge of the unknown.

Haud ma Chips, Ah've Drapped the Wean! Glesca Grannies' Sayings, Patter and Advice

Allan Morrison
Illustrated by Bob Dewar
ISBN 978-1-908373-47-2 PBK
£7.99

In yer face, cheeky, kindly, gallus, astute; that's a Glesca granny for you. Glesca grannies' communication is direct, warm, expressive, rich and often hilarious.

'Oor doctor couldnae cure a plouk oan a coo's erse.'

'That wan wid breastfeed her weans through the school railings.'

'Yer hair looks like straw hingin' oot a midden.'

'Ah'm jist twenty-wan an' ah wis born in nineteen-canteen.'

'The secret o' life is an aspirin a day, a wee dram, an' nae sex oan Sundays.'

Glesca grannies shoot from the mouth and get right to the point with their sayings, patter and advice. This book is your guide to the infallible wisdom of the Glesca granny.

Should've Gone Tae Specsavers, Ref!

Allan Morrison
Illustrated by Bob Dewar
ISBN 978-1-908373-73-1 £7.99

The referee. You can't have a game without one. The most hated man (or woman) in football but you have to invite one to every game.

Enjoy a laugh at the antics and wicked humour of Scottish referee Big Erchie, a powerhouse at five foot five, and a top grade referee who strikes fear into the hearts of managers and players alike as he stringently applies the laws of the game.

But Big Erchie is burdened with a terrible secret... He's a Partick Thistle supporter.

Details of these and other books published by Luath Press can be found at: **www.luath.co.uk**

Luath Press Limited
committed to publishing well written books worth reading

LUATH PRESS takes its name from Robert Burns, whose little collie Luath (*Gael.*, swift or nimble) tripped up Jean Armour at a wedding and gave him the chance to speak to the woman who was to be his wife and the abiding love of his life.

Burns called one of 'The Twa Dogs' Luath after Cuchullin's hunting dog in Ossian's *Fingal*. Luath Press was established in 1981 in the heart of Burns country, and now resides a few steps up the road from Burns' first lodgings on Edinburgh's Royal Mile.

Luath offers you distinctive writing with a hint of unexpected pleasures.

Most bookshops in the UK, the US, Canada, Australia, New Zealand and parts of Europe either carry our books in stock or can order them for you. To order direct from us, please send a £sterling cheque, postal order, international money order or your credit card details (number, address of cardholder and expiry date) to us at the address below. Please add post and packing as follows: UK – £1.00 per delivery address; overseas surface mail – £2.50 per delivery address; overseas airmail – £3.50 for the first book to each delivery address, plus £1.00 for each additional book by airmail to the same address. If your order is a gift, we will happily enclose your card or message at no extra charge.

Luath Press Limited
543/2 Castlehill
The Royal Mile
Edinburgh EH1 2ND
Scotland

Telephone: 0131 225 4326 (24 hours)
email: sales@luath.co.uk
Website: www.luath.co.uk